THE WEDDING DIARIES

THE WEDDING DIARIES

HOW TO GET MARRIED IN STYLE
WITHOUT
BREAKING THE BANK

LAURA BLOOM

EDITORS: RICHARD CRAZE, RONI JAY

Published by White Ladder Press Ltd
Great Ambrook, Near Ipplepen, Devon TQ12 5UL
01803 813343
www.whiteladderpress.com

First published in Great Britain in 2005

10 9 8 7 6 5 4 3 2 1

ISBN 0 9543914 8 9

British Library Cataloguing in Publication Data
A CIP record for this book can be obtained from the British Library.

Designed and typeset by Julie Martin Ltd
Cover design by Julie Martin Ltd
Printed and bound by TJ International Ltd, Padstow, Cornwall

WHITE LADDER PRESS
GREAT AMBROOK, NEAR IPPLEPEN, DEVON TQ12 5UL
01803 813343
WWW.WHITELADDERPRESS.COM

To Pop and Nannan

and to Marjorie

We miss you

Others, dear girl, may wish thee wealth,
I wish thee bliss and rosy health,
Health and bliss to make thee say,
Happy was my bridal day

Verse on Victorian wedding favour

Acknowledgements

In the writing of this book, I firstly want to thank my husband, Laurence. He tolerated my pre-wedding stress like an absolute hero (well, almost all of the time). He then had to relive all the agony by reading my manuscript night after night in bed and offering his honest critique – not a nocturnal habit I recommend to other newlyweds. I am also grateful to my sister Lorraine Howell of Rensascent Design for taking time to read an early draft and for all her help and hard work on our wedding plans.

Thanks also to Roni Jay and Richard Craze at White Ladder for their encouragement and enthusiasm.

Finally, thanks to *Your and Your Wedding* magazine for permission to use their 2004 survey and to all the many people and organisations who made our wedding the best day of our lives.

Contents

Introduction

Congratulations! You're getting married – or someone you know is getting married and you want to help him or her. Good for you. Naturally, you want it to be the best wedding ever. Romantic symbols flood into your mind – the dresses, the flowers and the age old traditions. Or maybe you want a wedding with a funky theme or a family bash that expresses both of your unique personalities? Yet, like a loose thread in that hand embroidered gown, something is worrying you. Weddings are the ultimate expression of romantic, eternal love – but also a byword for lavish conspicuous consumption. The price of a wedding is escalating each year: your parents probably spent a few hundred pounds but in 2004 the average cost of a wedding had escalated to £15,764[1]. Like every other aspect of life, expectations are rising as couples struggle to organise and pay for the most expensive day of their lives.

This book is intended to help you learn about weddings the fast and easy way. I made mistakes; I let the stress get to me and made the crucial error of trying to do far too much myself. Yet, as a couple, we also hit some of the high points of our lives. And we had a truly fabulous, classic wedding day for a fraction of the average spend.

Some of my tips and advice may not apply to you. This is not,

[1] All average costs from *'You and Your Wedding'* magazine survey 2004

for example, a guide to alternative ceremonies, same sex rites or weddings abroad – there are plenty of other sources of information freely available on every type of wedding you can imagine. My focus is largely on the preparations and planning for a traditional wedding. Even if you are planning this kind of wedding, some aspects of the book may not appeal to you. Ignore them. That is my wedding philosophy – make it your once in a lifetime day, unique to you and your vision. Nevertheless, I guarantee that some of the money saving ideas, planning tools and stress out stories will leave you wiser and more able to cope in the run up to your own wedding.

My years of working as a personnel and training manager did help me approach wedding planning as a logical problem solving exercise – but even the most meticulous plans didn't save me from sanity-threatening stress. A great wedding needs far more than meticulously filed To Do lists. The tears, the arguments, frustrations and sheer thrill of the undertaking are what make getting married one of the last great rites of passage. You and your beloved are about to make a huge public statement of your love and you may feel a paranoid level of scrutiny about everything from the height of your hairstyle to the shade of the icing on your cake.

The truth is that your guests are not a bunch of lifestyle makeover critics but a team of supporting fans, cheering you on with love and happiness on this special day. Plans and timetables are important but in the end, as you read my journal, you'll see that getting married is an emotional roller coaster. I hope to help you cope with those stomach churning descents into needless worry and panic – as well as giving you a foretaste of the dizzying highs that made the run up to my own wedding the most thrilling and proud year of my life.

I WILL, I WILL

WEDNESDAY 1ST JANUARY

The first day of the year and at last it's the year of our wedding! It's a beautiful day bursting with frosty sunshine, like a good omen of bright, bright days to come. Our church wedding is booked for 30th August, so that's a whole eight months of beautiful, blissful wedding preparations to look forward to. Well, that's what the bridal industry promises, isn't it? Whirlwind tours of glamorous couturiers where I'll be draped like a princess in spangled organza or tucked and boned into sculptured brocades. Eight months of diamonds, tulle, rosebuds, champagne, and those adorable little silk tied parcels inscribed with our entwined initials. Well, I can forget that straight away. Our whole budget is a cringeworthy £2,500. How can I pull of a wonderful wedding on such a tiny budget? And it will be wonderful, it must be wonderful – if one woman's planning and perspiration can pull it off.

Personally, I might have chosen the wedding abroad option (any excuse for a holiday) but Laurence stopped me in my tracks with the first of his amazing pronouncements – no, he wanted a church wedding. Then he said he wanted it to be small and informal. Perhaps he doesn't realise the utter contradiction involved in Church Wedding vs Small and Informal? Third and finally, he suggested a contribution of £1,500 towards the budget. As I had another thousand stashed away, we've got the miniscule total of £2,500 for our whole church wedding.

So, meet Laurence. He's 38, clever, fair haired and handsome (to me especially) and works as a lecturer in digital photography. Beneath his calm and conscientious exterior he's a mix of art student bohemian, lover of serious books and ideas, and 100% loyal romantic. He's also as daft as a brush in his private moments, which is one of the million reasons I love him. And finally, he's what he describes as 'sensible' with money. In other words, there's a long standing joke amongst his family that they'll have to bring their own sandwiches, if he ever gets married. Over my dead body.

We met via the internet in 1999 and our first date was literally a melding of two soulmates; I knew we would be together forever. We found we loved the same books and music, that we are both the youngest of three (him of three brothers, me of three sisters) and even our names, Laura and Laurence, echo rather spookily. Three weeks after we met we were in Prague, and since then we've journeyed and eaten our way around a fair amount of the globe, got engaged after his proposal at Aphrodite's Rock in Cyprus, bought a house and here we are – both wanting to be married but not at all sure about how to go about this wedding lark.

Problem Number One (the only one we've addressed so far) was finding a venue. We've bought a house together in the beautiful village of Dodleston in Cheshire. The village has a delightful and ancient church but no obvious venue to wine and dine our guests afterwards.

A Place For Us

Venues

Choosing your venue is inextricably linked to the final cost, atmosphere and visual impact of your wedding. Do you want to spend your whole day at 'Approved Premises' or have a religious or civil wedding followed by a party elsewhere?

1 ***Combined Ceremony and Celebration***

There are over 4,000 approved premises in the UK with proposed legislation likely to make many more available in the future. From zoos to sports grounds to orangeries and castles, it's less hassle for your guests and of course less of a logistics battle for you. Disadvantages can be:

- Conveyer belt services with rent-a-wedding backdrops in a bland function room.
- Complex pricing structures that can tie you into in-house caterers and suppliers.

Country house hotels: about £500 plus £200+ ceremony fee
Small castle or stately home: day hire starts at £3,000
Top historical properties – wedding package including food and accommodation: start from about £10,000

2 ***Separate ceremony and celebration***

The ceremony

A legally recognised ceremony must be conducted by:

- A Registrar at a civil ceremony in a Registry Office or approved premises, or
- A minister of a recognised religion at an appropriate location approved for marriage.

Registry Office wedding: about £100
Church wedding: around £200

> *Post-ceremony celebration*
> After dealing with the legalities at a civil ceremony or religious venue, there are no limits but your imagination on the venue for a party:
> *At home or someone else's home: nil*
> *A restaurant: bill plus optional small charge*
> *Anywhere from art galleries, boats, country houses, theme parks, to the top of a mountain: just check with the owners and pay as appropriate*

Reluctantly deciding against our own village, I started to search further afield. Then, after a few week's internet frenzy, Laurence made another Big Pronouncement. He hated hotels. He had been to too many dreadful hotel weddings. Another few days of obsessive search continued with nothing appealing, save for a few hours wasted daydreaming about remortgaging the house to hire a medieval castle. Then, one night as I stared at another dreary hotel banqueting room on the computer screen, a potentially perfect site surfaced from my frazzled unconscious.

It was a warm sultry evening last summer and Laurence was teaching his evening class. Jumping in the car I set out for Eccleston, a tiny but quintessentially lovely village on the edge of the Duke of Westminster's estate, where his former workers live in fairy tale houses and barley-twist chimneyed cottages. At the centre of the village is a vast High Gothic church replete with the Duke's coat of arms on the golden gates and a stunning avenue of lime trees leading to the oak doors. Laurence had taken me to see the village when we first met and it has a dreamlike quality, a mixture of half-timberered black and white Grimm's Fairyland and the surreal Englishness of Alice In Wonderland. Of course there are no pubs, hotels or guest houses, so like our own village it lacks any obvious venue for the reception. Yet – I had just remembered that by the meadows stretching down to the River Dee stands a long, low building with a lawn at the rear. A small sign answered my wish – *Village Hall.* It looked perfect. Peering in, I could see that it was stark and plain but had a stage, a high beamed roof and a kitchen to the rear. Perfect. With timing that now seems destiny, I strolled up to the church to find a friendly middle-aged man exercising a huge wolfhound. I had bumped into Jonathan, Rector of Eccleston, and his dog Lupus. Jonathan showed me around the impressive church and I knew I had in one stroke found a combination of church, reception venue and kindly and like minded minister. Within two weeks we had booked the church for our wedding and I had an agreement for hire of the village hall for the modest sum of £200. So, the one document I have ready to file in my purple folder is the contract for our venue, written out in beautiful copperplate lettering.

THURSDAY 2ND JANUARY

It's now more than six months since that booking and I have nothing else to show for it. No dress, no caterer, no photographer, nothing. After our first shared Christmas together in our new house it's time to make some resolutions:

NEW YEAR'S RESOLUTIONS

I will (sounds very wedding-like already)

- Organise wedding in calm and professional manner as befits former personnel and training manager
- Lose one stone (to look curvy but not fat in wedding dress)

- Begin proper beauty routine (on sudden nightmare realisation should have done this since puberty or even birth)
- Go to gym three times a week and draw motivation from focusing on wobbling bits in mirrors
- Share beautiful, exciting wedding preparations with Laurence
- Subtly persuade Laurence to prepare wedding in my own meticulously pre-planned way
- Motivate fab team of helpers so I can simply drift through preparations in zen like calm
- Keep to £2,500 budget
- Win loads of bridal competitions as only possible way to stick to budget
- Use our wedding to show how much we love everyone

I won't

- Get ridiculously stressed out like typical neurotic brides
- Eat usual diet of deadly dull low fat food supplemented by thrilling high fat gastronomic experiments
- Lose more than 1 stone, to avoid turning into haggard Miss Haversham lookalike
- Be intimidated by mad looking ancient harpie like wedding shop assistants
- Behave like natural scruff, but instead project radiant image of young at heart bride to be
- Use credit cards for wedding day magnificence resulting in married life of debt and misery
- Leave *anything* to the last minute
- Bake my own wedding cake (definitely)

- Let anyone upset me
- Have a wedding like anyone else's ever in the whole history of the universe

I've invested in a new purple folder with *Wedding: 30th August* written in wonky biro on the spine and packed it with bundles of empty plastic sheets. I've also invested in a huge blue concertina file marked with little tabs I've optimistically completed called *Stationery, Ceremony, Food* and *Outfits.* And, of course I've got this brand new Memories Journal with a whole doorstep of scarily blank pages. Turning to the white expanse of page marked 30th August I feel a chill settle on me even colder than the icy swirls decorating our windows. Disaster or dream day? It just doesn't bear contemplation.

FRIDAY 3RD JANUARY

Off to Manchester today and feel like a real life genuine engaged couple who are actually going to get married. We look at arts and crafts fabrics at the Sanderson shop and at Kendals. Together we choose fabric samples for our kitchen blind and for the first time in my life I feel like half of a couple in a light romantic comedy, all hand in hand and wonderfully smug. Can't believe these simple bits and bobs are so nice to do because we're doing them together.

Tonight, emboldened by our fabric selection success, I mention some catering menus to Laurence and he asks to see them. Although we normally talk like two adults of equal status, anything about the wedding turns me into a simpering child on tenterhooks and this in turn changes him into some kind of stern and serious lawgiver.

The catering really is the biggie as regards my foodie family but it will involve Big Spending – not an easy subject to raise with Laurence. Thankfully, Laurence agrees that the menus look promising. We brainstorm our guests' requirements and agree the meal has to provide:

1 A good selection of modern vegetarian food for our friends
2 A good selection of old-fashioned plain food for older family members
3 Non-fish, non-nut and diabetic options
4 Absolutely no beef paste sandwiches
5 Somehow, simultaneously, all of this has to be – well, very cheap
6 The result is I've fixed up an appointment on Wednesday 8th January with Country Cuisine's manager, Leonie.

TEAM MANAGEMENT

GETTING OTHERS ORGANISED

Choosing a supplier is another crucial decision. Treat it as if you are recruiting to the very important job it is – your assistant on the most important day of your life:

1 *Jot down a job description considering*

- *Proximity:* geographical area and ease of face to face communication.
- *Expertise*: specialist in weddings or generalist supplier, any specialised skills and services required.
- *Experience*: how long in business, experience with similar weddings.

2 *Cast your net*

- Ask around for recommendations.

- Consult Yellow Pages, bridal journals, trade magazines and directories.
- Visit stands at bridal fairs.
- Request menus, price lists, brochures and samples.

3 ***Shortlist***

- For crucial suppliers like wedding organisers or caterers, arrange to meet at least 2–3 suppliers who have impressed you so far.
- Ask probing questions about every aspect of their service and who exactly will deal with queries and deliver on the day.
- Try to sample, test and taste the goods or services on offer.

4 ***Select***

- Confirm your decision in writing immediately.
- Let any also-rans know too, as they may hold the date.

TIP: *If you feel uneasy about any way in which you are treated, forget that supplier and move on down the list.*

Saturday 4th January

The trouble with doing anything about the wedding is that my brain goes into an overdrive of wedding mania and I can't sleep. So, after talking menus for a while, we switch off the light, Laurence drops off and I go into major planning mode. The bedroom ceiling is suddenly lit up with schemes, plans and budgets. After an hour of pointless prevarication between spinach roulade and ratatouille tart, I get up and read in the spare bedroom. I can't help but feel this is self-defeating as every hour I spend awake after midnight leaves me more tired and raggy when I should be doing some energetic wedding arranging in the real world.

Later, on a long walk in wintry Delamere Forest, Laurence is deathly quiet. Even worse, when I try to coax out the problem he just says, very bluntly, that he doesn't want to talk to me. Charming! This mood only grips him about once a year and I've learned from his previous attacks of The Grumps that it really is best to leave him alone. Yet, as we stomp around the primeval Mere in our boots and scarves I'm forced to think about our relationship as tears foolishly spring up in my eyes. The wedding may well put a very big strain on us. Laurence is, to put a name on it, ambivalent. He wants to get married, yet having reached that decision he is barely tolerating much that goes with it. "I don't want any fuss," is one of his favourite quotes. "I hate being the centre of attention," is another. So I'm going to have to tread carefully with my wonderful, mixed up, sensitive fiancé.

We get home and there's a message from Laurence's solicitor on the phone. The sale of his old house in Chester has gone through and I tease him he's suddenly a man of fortune very much worth marrying. The mood lightens. He was just worried about the sale of his house. It's such a pity that all that lovely dosh can't be blown on the wedding. Yet, surely, it must help us out a teensy, little bit?

SUNDAY 5TH JANUARY

Church now beckons as we attend at least every couple of weeks in order to be admitted onto the electoral roll at Eccleston. Today there is a spectacular frost and we drive past fields and copses etched in silver. We enjoy going to church and have got into the habit of discussing Jonathan's sermons. I also love the formality, the intense beauty of the church and quietly thinking about others for just one peaceful hour in the week.

THE WEDDING SERVICE

How Much Does A Church Wedding Cost?
Church fees for a marriage service: about £150-200
Publication of banns: £18
Marriage certificate: £3.50

In addition, if you live outside the parish:
Banns certificate from your own parish: £27
A common licence (exempting from Banns): £62

Many ministers encourage couples from outside their parish to gain admittance onto the church's electoral roll by means of attendance over a specified period. From around 2007 it is likely that weddings will be permitted at any Anglican church where a couple can show a 'demonstrable connection' such as having been baptised there.

A quick trip to see some bathroom fittings to replace our grotty bathroom and then I'm off on wedding business again, to a bridal fair in Chester. I find the whole event and my reactions extremely odd. At 36, I'm what you might call a mature bride. Despite being far too grown-up to admit it to friends, I suppose this wedding fulfils some kind of stifled, secret dream. Women of my age grew up post-punk (marriage is political oppression), and post-feminist (marriage is just unspeakable). I had my independence, my career and even my son, Chris, without any neanderthal

oppression from a man, thank you very much. Maybe, like feminist Gloria Steiner who just got married at 63, it's a case of marriage having grown up just as much as I have. It's about equality, sharing, partnership – and well, let's face it, romantic vows of love and wearing 50 metres of embroidered tulle. It's strange, very strange.

The bridal show strikes me as something between a Christmas pantomime and a toy store for grown-ups. There is an excruciating toastmaster (not even to be contemplated), and a loud and nasal soprano. Next, a deeply fascinating fashion show at which the models are all real life brides wearing their own made-to-measure wedding dresses. I am amazed at the way some girls have chosen dresses that simply do not suit them. Extreme dresses, such as medieval bat wing affairs, look bizarre rather than beautiful. Also, many of these young bods do not suit the current fashion for strapless gowns and noticeably droop around the bosom. And these are slender, willowy twenty-somethings, not curvy hourglass 38Cs like me. I do in fact make myself a promise *never* to have a dress hand made for myself. Why? I feel it is far less risky to choose a finished dress, try it on and see immediately how it sits than to gamble on a seamstress's skills.

DRESS FOR SUCCESS

ATTIRE

Bridal attire comes in five main varieties:

1 Outfits not specifically designed for weddings: evening dresses, trouser suits, in fact anything you fancy
   - *Vintage evening dress: £50-300*
   - *Off-the-peg evening dress: £100-300*

2 Home-sewn wedding dresses
Sew Bridal magazine publishes McCall, Butterick and Vogue patterns: *about £4+ materials*

3 Off-the-peg wedding dresses
- *Department store 'designer' tagged dress: £300-500*
- *Traditional satin gown with train: from £400-1,000*
- *Highly worked bridal store gown: £1,000+*

4 Made to measure wedding dresses from a bridal house
- *Made to measure based on a cotton toile used as a template for the final gown: from around £1,000-2,000*

5 Made to measure wedding dresses from a couture designer
- *Unique to you couture styling: £2,000+*
  - *Average Spend on wedding dress: £913*

Chatting to the woman sitting beside me, we find we both feel the same about the models. Karen is a mature bride like me and is getting married in less than four months' time. Amazingly, she has hardly prepared anything yet. She is getting married for the second time, to a man she has met on the Friends Reunited website – though to be fair, I think she had already split up with her first husband. This wedding is to be on such a tight budget it makes me and Laurence sound like Posh and Becks. She rattles off some of the amazing bargains she has picked up – a £10 veil from Bhs and £5 slabs of plain white iced Christmas cake from Asda to serve as wedding cake. I admire her budgeting skills but am a bit aghast at having such a complete penny bazaar of a wedding.

GETTING ORGANISED

BRIDAL FAIRS

- Bridal fairs are the most time effective way to find out what goods and services are available in your locality.
- From cake samples to fashion shows and displays of favours, this is your chance to give suppliers the third degree about prices and availability.
- Pick up a carrier bag for bundles of brochures, free magazines and price lists to study at leisure and use on pinboards.
- Local Fairs are a wonderful opportunity to link up with other local brides and check out their best buys and recommendations.
- Prize draws will have good odds but may result in 'You have won 10% off a dress fitting' phone calls.

  – *Local bridal fairs at hotels and venues: free or up to £5*

  – *National Wedding Events: about £10*

An impressive woman photographer gives me a quote of about £500 for a pared down album of simple reportage photos. A florist suggests a similar sum for flowers. Then I find a chocolate truffle cake in my dream covering – white chocolate curls. Yet another £500. By now the real bride models are drunkenly swaying in the foyer with fags and champagne in hands and I can feel the tantrums brewing. Going home I feel like I've smuggled something slightly nasty and addictive into the house as I stuff the glossy brochures down the side of my armchair before Laurence can see them. The prices have been a shock – and I'm disappointed at how few prize draws there were. Having discovered the prices of everything, I'm just not sure how to make our budget stretch.

Wednesday 8th January

Big day today as I hope to get the catering sorted out. As a very keen cook I have been tempted to self cater. It's only after I've thought hard about the logistics of mass food preparation that I give up on that idea.

The Wedding Feast

Catering With Style

Doing it Yourself

- May be tempting but will require military style planning and drilling of friends and family to clean up, heat up, serve up and clear up.
- Ready made dishes from shops make a sensible compromise but often have short shelf lives and require responsible chilling:
  Supermarket antipasti selection (cured meat and olives) serves 12: from £17
  Ready-made sushi party pack serves 8-10: from £30
  Supermarket panna cotta – 5 portions: £5
  Swan ice sculpture: from £25
- The chief argument against self-catering is the risk of food poisoning in a warm environment.
- As when recruiting professionals, ask yourself whether your mum or Auntie Bertha has catered on this scale, to your desired standard, consistently over time. No? Politely decline, insisting that you want everyone to relax and enjoy your day with you.
- Don't forget that catering for large numbers requires vast equipment, gigantic serving dishes, crockery, cold storage, transport and clearing.

- If you opt to do it yourself, consider predominantly cold food. For example, for a reception with a barn dance you could provide a very upmarket ploughman's.

Once Leonie arrives, I'm immediately impressed with her professional manner and enthusiasm for cooking. We both share a passion for collecting recipes and commiserate with each other over failing to find the perfect method of storing our recipe clippings.

Based on my previous experience as a personnel manager I know a checklist is essential. After all, it's bad practice to ring candidates after an interview with a series of questions you forgot to ask. We settle down with coffees and I make notes on my writing pad:

Q: Can you tell me about your catering experience?

A: *We have very busy contracts with local training providers and do lots of weddings in various locations. We haven't worked at Eccleston but I have heard it's a lovely venue. I would need to visit it closer to the time but I'm sure it will be fine.*

Q: What facilities do you need?

A: *A kitchen, storage, cooker and fridges are useful but not essential. We have even catered for weddings in marquees in the middle of flooded fields! We use a chiller van and much of the food is pre-prepared at our unit just before we set off.*

Q: What about waiting staff? How many would you suggest for 50 guests?

A: I would use five to six staff, with at least one just washing up. They would wear smart black and white.

Q: Are you prepared to serve our own wine and soft drinks? Do you charge corkage?

A: *Yes, we can serve it but we will need to buy ice to chill the wine.*

We can supply the glasses and waitress service and won't charge corkage. We suggest Buck's Fizz to start, red and white wine, water, champagne for the toast and soft drinks or beers as it's summer. We don't recommend you supply spirits or any very strong alcoholic drinks. Punches and Pimms are notoriously strong and can be quite messy.

Q: The hall has plenty of trestle tables but the plastic chairs aren't quite right. Can you supply furniture?

A: *Yes, we would suggest hiring round tables for a wedding. The trestle tables will be useful for the buffet. I can send you details of furniture suppliers. We can also supply all your linen direct.*

Q: Can you make a chocolate wedding cake for us? Can you serve it as a dessert?

A: *No, I'd rather not make the cake* (shame). *If you supply it we could serve it with summer fruits and we also supply Cheshire Farms ice cream.*

Q: From your experience, what do you suggest regarding timings of the meal?

A: *Everything takes longer than you expect. For a 3pm ceremony we would serve the meal at 4.30pm to 5pm after photos and drinks. You will find things simply flow one into another. I would like someone specific I can liase with on the day over timings who isn't you, so we don't have to disturb you.*

Q: What about entertainment? What do you find works at a wedding?

A: *When I got married we had a big soul band and they got everyone up to dance. Also, I do suggest having some background music while eating the meal as sometimes the sound of cutlery on plates is a little off-putting if it takes a while for guests to relax. If you do have music in the evening, I could supply a cheese board, grapes and celery from*

Chester's Cheese Shop for a nominal charge. We had this at my own wedding and it is very popular and not as expensive as another, probably unnecessary, evening buffet.

Q: Do you have any references I can see?

A: *Yes.* (Leonie shows me a bundle of thank you cards and letters. They are glowing and words like 'quality', 'superb' and 'compliments' stand out. One card describes the catering as being like the film 'Babette's Feast' with one delicious course after another. Mmmm.)

Q: How much time will you need to set up?

A: *As the food is prepared off site we can set up the previous day. We just need the final guest numbers a few weeks before the event.*

Finally, I choose a menu with a waitress served choice of starters, a huge buffet main course served one table at a time, followed by waitress served dessert and coffee:

MENU

WARMED GOAT'S CHEESE CROSTINI

WITH ROCKET AND CARAMELISED ONION

OR

TOMATO AND BASIL SOUP

•••

SUPREME OF SALMON WITH THAI MARINADED KING PRAWNS

ROAST BEEF FILLET WITH PARSLEY OIL AND HORSERADISH

LEMON CHICKEN

SPINACH ROULADE

RATATOUILLE TART

•••

HOT NEW BABY POTATOES IN BUTTER AND PARSLEY

GREEN SALAD

TOMATOES, FETA CHEESE AND MARINADED OLIVES DRIZZLED WITH TUSCAN OLIVE OIL AND BASIL

CARROT AND CORIANDER SALAD

STEAMED ASPARAGUS

•••

A SELECTION OF SPECIALITY BREADS

•••

CHOCOLATE WEDDING CAKE

SELECTION OF RED SUMMER FRUITS WITH

CHESHIRE FARMS ICE CREAM OR FRESH CREAM

•••

COFFEE AND MINTS

All of this sounds very promising but I'm still on tenterhooks as Leonie will send me a quote for the costs.

Feeling a little more pleased with myself I shoot off to the gym where I'm getting stuck into a new routine. I've got a little green card with my fitness programme listed and I'm trying to increase my minutes and reps each week. Today I manage 12 minutes on the bike, seven minutes on the cross-trainer, seven minutes on the steps, 10 minutes on the treadmill plus some abs exercises on the mat and some stretches. So, today I get a gold star for effort – I've stuck to my diet, taken exercise, and I've made progress on the wedding. Big pat on the back.

THURSDAY 9TH JANUARY

I've designated Thursday afternoon as my indulgence time – a Pilates session at the health club to stretch my dodgy spine and attempt relaxation followed by shopping in Chester. This week I pick up a pretty diamante tiara from Bhs that's so cheap (£15) that it hardly matters if I change my mind. I've also snapped up a dozen half-price gold tealight holders (50p each) at Wilkinson's post-Christmas sale.

DRESS FOR SUCCESS

HEADDRESSES

A bridal headdress is the irresistible touch that turns any bride into a Princess:

- The headdress should complement your dress, ie Romantic (gilt crown), Hollywood (feathers) or Tropical (orchids).
  Tiara – high street: £10-100
  Feather haircomb: about £30
  Wide brimmed hat with feathers and veil: about £50 to hire
  Handmade 'designer' tiara: £100+
- Veils are optional these days: longer veils in a finer fabric will tend to hang better on the day. Remember you will need practice with your hairdresser to pin and position it.
  Veil – high street: from £10-100
  Floor length ivory veil – bridal specialist: from £100
  Average spend on veil and headdress: about £170

Next, I amble past the local Mecca of bridal wear – the Bridal House of Chester. Since setting our wedding date I've not yet had the courage to go into a bridal shop. The Bridal House takes up a large swathe of a Georgian Row, complete with old-fashioned georgette ruffles at the upper windows behind which I can spy walls bursting with dresses. The cream arches of the shop window frame a rigid tableau of ancient plasterwork mannequins dressed in a variety of gowns – maribou trimmed, sequinned and heavily embroidered. Resolved to keep my plastic undisturbed, I go inside. Thick carpets muffle my scuffed boots as I dive upstairs to the hallowed Precincts of the Bride. My heart is actually racing as I find myself facing a glass cabinet of bridal shoes. Did raggedy Cinderella ever feel quite as unworthy as me? Yet, it is heaven to see gorgeous wedding shoes close up. I recognise Rainbow Shoes as a brand that are not only pretty objects of ivory satin desire, but are also blissfully comfortable. And as my feet, like the rest of me, are not quite pristine and virginal (rather, notoriously achey) finding the bridal version of comfy slippers is something like nirvana.

Emboldened, I enter the bridal area and am surrounded by rail after rail of billowing ivory satin, silk, lace and taffeta. Darting past two chatting assistants I handle some of the fabrics. They are so heavy and so complicated, and have such surprising laces, trains, crossovers and ruffles, that only the initiated must know how to fathom their mysteries. The price tags are actually not too terrifying – £500, £764, shop soiled £250. This is the Sale section but I still haven't a clue where to start.

Meanwhile, I earwig as a small and decidedly round young customer appears.

"First fitting?" An assistant picks up a huge leather bound ledger and spreads it over a narrow wooden counter that must have been part of the original Georgian fittings. "Just the deposit today, thanks. That'll be £500."

Five hundred? I quail with fear. Five hundred *deposit?*

The round young woman hands over a credit card and I think about the time it's going to take her to pay that off – and wonder how much more it's going to cost her in accessories, shoes and all the rest.

"And the bridesmaids are booked in for Saturday at 3pm?" The girl nods and I think – why don't you just hand over all your plastic, your next year's salary and eternal soul and be done with it all in one go?

Annoyingly, just as I'm mulling this over, the other assistant bears down towards me.

"Are you looking for a dress?"

"Er, yes. But not yet. I don't need it yet. I'm just looking."

"Any type in mind?"

I had just been pawing a goldish creation with a pearl encrusted bolero. I drop it like it was woven by genetically modified silk-worms.

"Something plain," I try weakly. "Something –," I mime 'slimming' by moving my fingernails in a straight line down my torso but say, "with a corset type bodice." She nods.

"But nothing too –," I want to say 'fetish like' but remember I'm in a bridal shop where I suppose they make you wash your mouth out with perfume if you hint at the unwholesome. She is waiting, watching me as I dither.

"Nothing too over the top," I manage.

Before I can stop her she's shot off to the rails and dragged a 10-ton creation in pure white with a boned strapless waist clincher.

"No," I say, cringing. "More cover. Good God. My arms."

Next comes something Scarlett O'Hara could have wowed them with down at the Dixieland Ball. A Very Big Skirt that could fly you to the moon on a windy day.

"No." I shake my head, aghast. "Straightish skirt?"

Mmm, the next one is nice but very low cut. My boobs would be bound to tumble out at the altar. The one after that is lovely. Cream satin, V-pointed bodice and straight skirt. I'm getting the hang of this. And miraculously, I do know what I want after all.

"Do you want to try it on?"

I catch sight of the tag. Seven hundred and fifty pounds.

"No," I mumble, grabbing my handbag.

"When exactly *is* the wedding?"

Ah, she's caught me now. In the Wedding World anything booked less than two years ahead is last minute. I blanch like a heretic at the Inquisition.

"Not till much later in the year," I gabble. "No. I'll be back though. I'm on a diet," I protest. "When I've lost weight I'll come back."

She holds up the dress which does look lovely and twinkles at me seductively. "We can easily alter it if you lose weight," she says winningly.

"Sorry, I've got to go." I almost run down the stairs to the chilly street. Still, mission accomplished. I have been inside a bridal shop. And I haven't spent a penny – yet.

6PM: Slimming World. Post-Christmas weigh-in. I've put on 3lbs since my last visit in December – not good, but not a complete disaster either, given all the cake, chocs and nice things I've shovelled down. That puts me a grand total of one stone over target. Nice round figure (sic) at least.

8PM: Competitions Club. Every month a group of us competitions addicts meet to swap tips, prize news and entry forms. My fellow compers are rooting for me to win wedding goodies and

Gwen, our founder member, gives me a local newspaper draw to win tickets to a bridal fair at Tatton Hall. As there are 50 tickets to give away the odds are good to win.

SUNDAY 12TH JANUARY

Having a lovely, lazy weekend with Laurence, just mooching, smooching, catching up with friends and each other. Now we have made some progress on the menu my mind has turned to ordering the drinks. A few years ago, I had a very lucky win of a 'Cellar of Wine' from Racing Green clothing. It in fact turned out to be an account with Berry Bros & Rudd, the wonderful London wine merchants. We ordered a few cases to celebrate, but when our wedding planning started I knew I had to leave it untouched.

Today I check the account and there is £545 left to spend on wedding wine. Not too bad, I think, for 50 people – after all, that's more than a tenner per person. However, when I tot up my wish list of pink champagne and loads of red and white wine it comes to £700. I'll need to cut that back as it's pointless overspending on wine when there are so many other things to overspend on…

While on the PC I do a quick secret search on bands. I haven't talked to Laurence about it yet but as we both like folk music the appeal of a Ceilidh is growing. It suits the village setting and will get everyone up and actively mixing. My quick net search has thrown up lots of local Ceilidh bands with snatches of music to listen to, reviews and pictures.

THURSDAY 16TH JANUARY

My friend Angela's seven year old daughter is to be my bridesmaid and today I email to confirm she hasn't changed her mind. She hasn't, and I'm feeling the pressure after telling Angela I want all the bridesmaid shopping done by June, such is my horror of anything last minute.

6PM: Lost just one lousy pound at Slimming World despite two sessions of Pilates, two big aerobic sessions and following the Slimming World diet (oh, except for wine and kiwi pud with friends and a very wicked white choc sundae at the pictures...).

MONDAY 20TH JANUARY

Very cheered to get Leonie's quote. For the menu we discussed she will charge £17.50 per head, which with VAT makes a round £20. I think £1,000 for 50 people is good and Laurence agrees. She has also given me loads of advice and costings for linen, furniture, etc. The post also brings a free ticket to Tatton Hall Wedding Fair, so thanks to Gwen for that. Nevertheless, I'm still grumpy. Thinking about it, my bad mood originates from a vile recurrent dream: it is noon on my wedding day and I have nothing to wear. I can't believe time has flown by so quickly. Someone tells me there is a wedding shop open but already it's early afternoon and nothing I try is quite right. The skirt I try on looks second-hand and tatty. Oh no, it's after 3pm already! Why, oh why didn't I get organised? I feel sick with self-loathing and wake up both relieved that it was a dream and horrified that I still haven't got a wedding dress.

STAYING SANE

WEDDING NIGHTMARES

Pre-wedding dreams about not having the right clothes are an almost universal anxiety dream. The message is clear – on a superficial level, get organised. On a deeper level, clothes represent our outer façade. Weddings are scary and suck us into deep uncertainties about how to present ourselves. Other common prenup nightmares are:

- You arrive at your wedding but there are other brides there outshining you.
  (Do you lack confidence in your groom's resistance to others?)
- A catastrophe, war or even murdering your parents.
  (The destruction of your old way of life in preparation for the new)

SATURDAY 25TH JANUARY

Today was momentous as Laurence paid off a huge sum (about half of our mortgage) with some of the proceeds of his house sale. It feels fantastic. Now that we have a really small monthly mortgage payment I just might have a little bit more of my own cash available for the wedding…

Calling in at the Cathedral Refectory for lunch reminded us both of my first visits to Chester when we first fell in love. I light a candle and we both feel incredibly happy.

SUNDAY 26TH JANUARY

Today's sermon was about the Marriage at Canaan and Jonathan kindly mentioned us as one of the couples getting married at Eccleston this year. Then he talked about weddings as times of feasting, sharing and celebration. This sermon is ideal for our wedding and Laurence agrees that I should ask Jonathan if he can talk along similar lines on our Big Day. He also agrees that a folk band would be a good idea, so I make some quiet progress today.

Finally, I flew off to Tatton for the Wedding Fair. A bit disappointing as I now realise bridal fairs attract almost all the same suppliers offering the same types of wares.

THURSDAY 30TH JANUARY

My life seems on a slide again. For some reason, when I take my Thursday off to relax I'm feeling sick and unwell. I've also had a misunderstanding with a publisher and another crashing disappointment over my yet to be published novel about Vivaldi. Then, I decided to try a makeover and instead of it being a nice, relaxing pampering session, it felt horrible. First of all the lady slapped a lot of ghoulishly pale foundation on my face. Next, when she dolloped a pinky brown colour on my eyes I looked like one of the Living Dead. The whole session was being videoed and later, when I watched it at home, I could see how twitchy I became. All afternoon, as I walked round Chester with the pallid mask of make-up on my face, I stooped my head like an extra from Michael Jackson's *Thriller*. Even my hair looks lank and the roots are showing through dark, so I need to get a hairdresser sorted out fast. To make matters worse, when I called at Slimming World I hadn't lost a pound. Felt horribly amazed and upset.

When Laurence got home from teaching his late class I told him I was fed up and he said "Come here, then," and opened his arms up wide. So I'm very lucky after all (muffled sob).

MUST DO:

Find miracle dress. Order tables and chairs (Gold? Not plastic). Lose weight (feed Laurence all fattening Christmas remains – but not creating bloater groom or early widowhood?) Buy lots of gold things, candles, etc, in post-Christmas sales. Get CDs and gig dates of bands. Talk to Laurence about a photographer (if no pictures why bother with all the rest?) Find cakemaker – preferably sugarcraft obsessive homeworker oblivious of hourly labour involved. Meet bridesmaid's mum to shortlist dresses. Find cheap honeymoon. Create youthful toned slim body (exercise, body brushing, diet, tablets, weights, scary electronic machines?) Create youthful wrinkle free clear complexion (drink water, cleanse, tone, retinol, exercises, primers, peels, stop smiling?) Talk to Laurence about snippets he needs to know about and censor all the rest to shield Beloved from stress. Find miracle hairdresser. Draw up list of guest accommodation. Win everything possible (quick, quick, before too late). Avoid stress. Make time for romance. Check diary. Period dates? Manipulate hormones? PMT? HRT???

LIST-MANIA

MONDAY 3RD FEBRUARY

Back down to earth today marking a pile of student assignments in my role as assessor to health management courses. Today I've been wilfully abusing all my innocent students' work by twisting it around to suit my own selfish ends. They have been answering questions on planning (in their cases, opthalmic services or opening new paediatric wards) but I've been trying to plan the wedding using the same theories:

1 ***What are you aiming to do?***

The idea here is to think very hard about the end result. Yes, we want a nice wedding but what does that mean? I try writing down our ideas in one sentence and come up with:

'We are trying to create a joyful, beautiful, stress free celebration of our marriage that involves, moves and relaxes our guests whilst fulfilling both my own and Laurence's ideas of a unique and personal day.'

TIP: *It is this vision of your wedding (whether a funky family rave up or cool, classy soiree) that you will need to hold onto when other people try to persuade you to do it their way.*

2 *What is the best way of doing it?*

'Stress free' is the key phrase that pops into my mind, as proved by my recurrent nightmare about everything being left to the last minute. I brainstorm a list of ideas around how to organise a wedding the stress free way:

- Start organising everything early with good quality bookings.
- Avoid last minute disappointments and chasing.
- Delegate and involve family friends (so everyone has a stake in the success of the day).
- Keep a folder of important documents and a diary planner.
- Make the day personal and unique to us.
- Help everyone know what is expected of them so they can relax and enjoy the day.
- Keep my head!

3 *What are you going to have to do?*

This is really my To Do list and it runs to pages and pages. All the jumble in my mind tumbles out like dusty old stuff bursting out from a neglected cupboard:

Choose a florist, order tables and chairs, buy garden tealights/flares, buy my outfit, finalise numbers and seating plans, organise Banns at local church, choose or make favours, send out invitations, and on and on and on...

TIME MANAGEMENT

GETTING ORGANISED

- The important thing is getting all of this down on paper – it's when there is too much floating in your head that anxieties build.
- Add other tasks as they occur to you over days, weeks and months.

- Keep a notepad by your bedside to jot down ideas if you wake in the night.
- Delegate tasks whenever possible.
- Use your diary to forward plan tasks for the next day, week and month.
- Start each day by visualising yourself achieving tasks successfully.
- 'Cluster' tasks into groups: an hour dedicated to phone calls and then an hour writing letters, is faster and more efficient than half-completing a jumble of tasks.

4 *When are you going to have to do them?*

Going through the list I schedule all the major tasks into chronological order. Soon I have proper lists of manageable tasks written under headings for each month. So now I have a To Do list for February comprising things I can happily get on with which don't depend on later events.

The result is that the remaining three quarters of my massive To Do list can be filed away under headings for April, May, June, July, August and Post-Wedding. Phew!

I also have an ongoing list of things that need a small but regular amount of time, such as entering wedding competitions and discussing ideas for hymns and readings with Laurence.

5 *What resources are we going to need?*

The main resources needed are Money, Time and Space.

Money

Since booking Leonie I've been feeling queasy. Our current projected budget looks like this (using 'E' to indicate estimates):

ESTIMATED BUDGET FEBRUARY 2003

	£
Hall hire	200
Furniture hire	E150
Catering	1000
Linen hire	E50
Cake	E100
Wine *(Competition win)*	540
Soft drinks/glass hire	E100
Band	E350
Wedding dress *(Mum to contribute)*	E300
Bridesmaid's dress	E100
Groom's suit hire	E150
Photography	E400
Flowers	E350
Stationery *(Home-made)*	Nil
Transport *(Brother-in-law's car)*	Nil
Ceremony	200
Wedding rings	E200
Honeymoon *(Luxury long weekend)*	E500
TOTAL	**4,690**
(SUBTRACT prize and guest contributions 840)	
TOTAL SPEND	**3,850**

It's no great surprise that the big problem is the budget. I have already overcommitted our spending by £1,350. Even if I add further savings to the kitty, I still need to be careful not to escalate our spending way beyond our means. Nevertheless, in my own optimistic way, I feel the predicted overspend could be worse.

Time

The resource that most people don't think about is time. I may be fortunate enough to be able to reschedule my work but Laurence has only a tiny amount of time (and mental energy) to deal with the arrangements. As he often jokes in a world of "money rich, time poor," he is sadly "money poor, time poor".

Nevertheless, when I look at scheduling tasks, even I have very little time in the final months and weeks. I'm going to have to be more hard headed about delegating to others.

Space

We are very short of space to store all the bits and pieces for the wedding. For example, with two already bursting wardrobes, where on earth can I store a dress? Then there are all the drinks and table decorations I intend to buy. The garage is our only storage area and that's too insecure to store crates of champagne.

6 *Review the plan – is it going to work?*

Finally, the theory stresses that a really robust plan has lots of input from lots of people. So I need to bounce my ideas around more openly with everyone – Lorraine, Laurence, Leonie, Jonathan, friends and family. The important thing about reviewing the plan is that it's flexible. If my ideas aren't going to work, or other people come up with better ideas, I'll have to change them.

Already I feel a lead cloak of worry lifting from my shoulders just because I've written this down. Taking the planning step by step makes it all seem so much more achievable. Yet at the same time I can't avoid the fact that some key steps need to be put in place *now*.

WEDNEDAY 5TH FEBRUARY

I can't believe how much better I feel. I can almost feel my halo lighting my way forward. During the day I've been thinking about all this delegation.

Who will do what – and when?

I need to mobilise people. Until now I have seen this as a one woman show but I need to be more like a movie director. I need to identify my cast, my props, script, stage directions and all the rest. Then I need to make sure everyone knows what they have to do beforehand and on the day itself. This feels a bit scary but I'm sure I've just stumbled on something crucial to getting the whole day to run successfully…

Do I have any 'champions' to help me? I've been playing around with a list of the key players and what their roles might be:

LAURENCE (GROOM) His role is to work with me on the planning, contribute to funding, attend the rehearsal, help set up the hall and deal directly with his best man, Keith. Oh, and marry me of course.

LORRAINE (DESIGNER) My sister's role is to design and decorate the village hall. She is also Leonie's contact on the day for any queries or questions. She is a ready made 'champion' and enthusiast.

KEITH (BEST MAN) Keith's role is to support Laurence, help set up the hall, attend the rehearsal, manage the ushers, manage money on the day, manage transport, attend to hire clothes and pick up the buttonholes. This sounds like a tremendous amount of work to dump on Keith, but I tell myself that it is the one job description entirely written by tradition so that the groom can enjoy a trouble free day.

CHRIS (GIVER AWAY) As my son Chris will be returning from his gap year travels in New Zealand his role is quite limited. He needs to choose an outfit, attend the rehearsal, travel in the car with me and actually give me away.

YVONNE, LIZ AND FRAN (USHERS) I like the idea of expanding the traditional male church usher role to include more female friendly roles like helping us decorate the hall, helping people to mix at the reception, passing around the guest book and organising the gift table. Fran is also our first aider.

NICK (DRIVER) Nick's role is to get me to the church on time in his gorgeous car.

JONATHAN (MINISTER) I hope he knows *his* role better than I do.

NICOLA (BRIDESMAID) As she is only seven years old Nicola's role is limited to attending the rehearsal and following me in church.

ANGELA (NICOLA'S MUM) Buying a dress and accessories will fall upon Nicola's mum. She will also need to attend the rehearsal.

I'm left with a number of roles still to cast. Firstly, we need a photographer who Laurence likes and trusts. Then, despite the fact that Laurence has insisted there are to be No Speeches, he has agreed to some friends reading poetry. I would like my eldest sister Marijke to read and my dad to play the piano. Poetry and music are important to us both so we need to think very carefully about the day's programme.

Finally, I remember another important person:

ME (BRIDE) My role is to direct The Plan, liase with everyone else, find a dress, find a cake, shoes, jewellery, make-up, sort out a photographer, arrange the Banns, write invitations, research accommodation, book a honeymoon, choose the wedding list, decide church seating, buy drink, etc, etc.

Mmm, it sounds like I'm back to where I started, only I've given myself the extra responsibility of co-ordinating a huge bunch of people as well as organise myself.

THURSDAY 6TH FEBRUARY

The usual routine with Pilates class (tiring) and then a trip to Marks & Sparks where I succeed in cantilevering myself into a pair of jeans *one size smaller.* Some kind of success, I reckon. Immediately afterwards, my confidence is shattered by the cruel Judgement of the Scales at Slimming World. I've put on 1lb. Honestly!

"But I've been going to the gym," I protest. I'm exasperated. "Nearly every day. Well, three times this week." I think of all those 20 minute slog outs on the cross-trainer and want to weep.

"Well, muscle is heavier than fat," admits the plumpy lady behind the desk.

That's no good to me. Even if I feel trimmer or more toned it just doesn't feel *virtuous* if I'm a whole pound heavier. I don't want to spend £3.75 a week to be patronised and depressed. I go to bed early, fed up.

FRIDAY 7TH FEBRUARY

A turnaround day. Confronting my To Do list head on, I get out the Yellow Pages and start connecting with people over the phone. First, I ring around for furniture hire prices. The main suppliers of furniture are marquee firms so I take a look at their wares:

A Place For Us

Venues

- Most marquee companies offer a bespoke service based on space available and guest numbers.
- Take advice on measurements so space is neither too cramped or too empty:
  9m x 12m marquee (120 people seated or 160 standing): around £1,300 plus delivery, VAT and optional extras
- Clarify exactly what extras you need:
  Parquet dance floor: from £100
  Heating: from £160
  White bistro chairs: from £1.20 each
  10 seater round table: from £7.50
  Lighting: from £150
  Fire extinguisher: £12
  Exit light: £25

Next, I make my first hair appointment. The hairdresser is situated in the Grosvenor Pulford Hotel, just a mile or two away from our village. The salon is smart and my hairdresser, Clare, is a cheery Welsh girl who regularly dresses the hair of brides who stay at the hotel.

"And what do you think makes a really good wedding?" I ask Clare.

"Well, I went to a friend's wedding," she chuckles, "and they had a Ceilidh band. It was such a laugh. Everyone got up and went mad dancing around. It can get a bit boring if everyone's just sitting around."

"And what about bridal hairstyles?" I ask after she's removed the highlighter foils and my long hair twinkles glamorously under the lights.

"Well, you could have it up or down, really. Just book in when you want a trial and bring along any pictures of styles you like. Oh, and bring your headdress along."

Mmm, my headdress. I wonder how the £15 Bhs tiara will bear up to close scrutiny. For £45 I can book a bridal hair trial and also have my hair dressed on the big day. I book in for the morning of the wedding at 10am. At last I can put a tick against something on my February To Do list.

BRIDAL BEAUTY

HAIRDRESSING

- Avoid fright wig syndrome by having a trial of each and every hairstyle that appeals.
- Snip pictures from magazines and brochures to show your hairdresser exactly what you would like him or her to attempt.
- Be flexible. Some styles may not be feasible for certain hair types.
- Get colour, condition and other treatments sorted out at least a month before the wedding. The week before is definitely not a time for shocking surprises.
- Try to be yourself only more beautiful – with shinier, twinklier, prettier hair.
- Hairdressing prices vary wildly:
  Mobile hairdresser in own home: from £20
  High Street bridal dressing: £40-100
  Celebrity hairdresser's magic scissors: Up to £500 per session

SATURDAY 8TH FEBRUARY

Off to my mum's where I show her a brochure from Slattery's patisserie and my dream white chocolate curl cake. She offers to pay for it, but at £300+ with delivery on top I just can't find it in myself to agree. "Maybe you could help me out with Chris's suit instead?" I ask. After all, it will cost at least £100 to hire or buy a suit for him.

My eldest sister Marijke rings and I broach the subject of a poem. "Just send it to me," she says and I wonder if she will think it's incredibly soppy. I've chosen a poem I read at Yvonne and Keith's handfasting called 'The Commitment Poem of the Pueblo Indian'. We also chat about accommodation, as she will be travelling up from London with her partner, David, and friend Julia. Only after booking our wedding ceremony did I find that 30th August is also Race Day in Chester and thousands of people will descend on the town for a flutter, a drink and a good time.

Marijke asks, "Have you told Dad yet that he isn't giving you away?" Clearly this is an issue. I'd better tackle it fast.

Finally, my mum reminds me that it was my dad's birthday last week. I forgot to even send a card. Am I really so wedding obsessed that I could forget my own dad's wedding? Sorry, slip of the fingers ...birthday. Says it all, really.

SUNDAY 9TH FEBRUARY

As Laurence says, today was an ideal Sunday. He brought his digital camera along to church and I realise he is quietly working on his own wedding plan – choosing images for the invitations. We also make a decision about one of our hymns. It is 'Be Thou My Vision,' an 8th Century Irish hymn that has been popularised in a beautiful version by Van Morrison. The words are wonderful, very simple, humble and apt.

Later we go for a long walk up aptly named Hope Mountain, a local beauty spot just over the border into Wales. Yvonne and Keith come with us and it's good to have company in the glorious winter sunshine high up on the hills. We chat about Yvonne and Keith's pagan handfasting last year, which perfectly illustrated their vision of the world. It was held at a small tented camp out in Wales on a stunning summer's day. Twelve friends and family gathered in a circle to read poems before the couple jumped over a broom and made their vows. Unconventional, romantic, last minute, unique – it was just wonderful and cost no more than a couple of hundred pounds. I do sometimes think Yvonne wonders what I'm making all this fuss about – that I should leave it all to just happen on the day. She also advises us strongly to take a honeymoon, as the comedown back to the kitchen sink on Monday morning after the weekend's excitement can be very depressing.

We have such an enjoyable talk about the wedding and they emphasise it's just a big party. Laurence also enthuses about us booking an Irish band and the idea of inviting a younger crowd in the evening. We finish the night with an Indian buffet in Chester and even then I am sensible and have a delicious but healthy vegetable curry. All in all, a great day combining fresh air and friends.

MONDAY 10TH FEBRUARY

Some new resolutions regarding the diet. While the pure Atkins sounds horrible, I have been trying the Dr Clarke diet by eating more protein and cutting down on carbs. Slimming World is clearly not working for me so I'll put my cash towards delicious protein like steaks and seafood.

After work I go in search of florists. The first shop I visit has an album of photos and some of the pictures are not especially pretty. It is easy to think that all weddings will look as perfect as the top class photography in the bridal magazines. The truth is that real life brides and grooms come in all shapes and sizes, and wear outfits that simply don't flatter or help them look their best.

I have a better experience at another florist inside a huge garden centre. The album is better; particularly interesting is a Vietnamese wedding at which the flowers are unusual and artful. Feeling bold, I ask to meet the florist. Sue is a direct and practical woman whose lean face animates when she talks about the pleasure of a challenging job. The price list she gives me sounds very reasonable:

'Country style' pew ends: from £12.50 each
Church pedestals: from £50 each
Rose buttonholes: from £5 each

I tot up the total cost of pew ends, pedestals, bouquets and buttonholes and discover it will be in the region of £300-400. Sue swings the order her way when she checks the date in her diary and tells me that the previous two Saturdays in August are already booked. Panicked, I give her my name and address.

Later, I ring Dad who seems unperturbed about his belated birthday card. I do, however, tell him that I've asked Chris to give me away. I explain that I would like everyone close to me to have a role and that as Chris is travelling from New Zealand I would like him to have the giver away role and my dad to play the piano. Ideally, I would love Dad to write something for the occasion as he is a wonderful composer but he seems rather reluctant. Dad makes it clear he would rather play something briefly in church than be 'the entertainer' at the reception.

FRIDAY 14TH FEBRUARY

A beautiful day. On first waking, we exchange Valentine's cards and kisses. For dinner I make a low carbohydrate feast: Thai crab cakes with chilli salsa, steak au poivre with swede mash and then tiramisu and strawberries. It is lovely to stay in and get quietly sozzled on red wine while the rest of the world battles for an overpriced table at a restaurant.

FRIDAY 21ST FEBRUARY

A visit from my bridesmaid Nicola and her mum, Angela, today. Nicola is a gorgeous little girl with flawless skin and innocent beauty. We look around Chester, avoiding the bridal houses as my plan is to try to find a dress for less than £100. I've considered the etiquette regarding who buys the dress and I know that it's only polite to foot the bill. At Debenhams the designer ranges are lovely and excellent value at around £50. Bhs also have new ranges that look very pretty but are a little stiffer and cheaper. We land out in Monsoon where there are the most gorgeous pink floral and chiffony dresses.

DRESS FOR SUCCESS

BRIDESMAIDS

The biggest impact on the cost of the bridesmaids after the number and where you source your dresses, is the age of your attendants. Big girls will tend to dictate what they want, unlike little ones:

Grown-up outfit
Purple sequin evening dress, department store: around £200
Purple hyacinth pomander: around £100
Jewelled shoes: up to £300

Child outfits
Lilac bridesmaid's dress, supermarket: £20
Fresh flower posy, local florist: £25
Ballerina shoes, high street: £10
Gold comb tiara, high street: £10

Looking at Nicola in the Monsoon dress I can see that it is perfect for a stylish London type wedding in a park with picnics and flower baskets. I have to remember that our church setting is very formal and my inclinations are moving from a simple gown and jacket towards a more formal wedding dress. So in the end, we decide to wait until I have chosen my dress and we can match that in shade and style.

Saturday 22nd February

Another set of friends to stay for the weekend, this time Ron and Hilary, two friends of Laurence's from his art college days, along with their lovely daughter Helen. After a busy day of walks and lively conversation I feel a bold idea bubbling up inside me and I ask Hilary if Helen would also like to be my bridesmaid. So now I have two gorgeous bridesmaids to dress and liase with, but there is a method to my madness. Helen is nine years old, stunning and

so self-assured and self-reliant that I am sure seven year old Nicola will enjoy her day far more with an older friend to guide her through the intricacies of the ceremony. They will also look absolutely beautiful together.

Hilary is also a fount of enthusiasm and information and recommends her friend John Mottershaw to be our photographer.

TUESDAY 25TH FEBRUARY

I have finally decided to hire seating for 70 from Events Solutions as our guest list of 50 seems to have a mushroom life of its own:

FURNITURE	
70 gold and burgundy spindleback chairs *(£1.95 each)*	£136.50
7 5ft 6 inch round tables *(£7.50 each)*	£52.50
1 3ft cake table	£6.00
Delivery and collection	£30.00
VAT:	£39.38
TOTAL	**£ 264.38**

While Laurence is teaching his evening class I attempt a prototype cake and my first ever chocolate curls. Using the best Belgian couverture white chocolate I temper it (raise and then cool the temperature to keep it glossy), spread it in a thin layer on a marble slab and then make about 40 perfect cigarette sized curls using a steel wallpaper scraper. Finally, I make some sticky white chocolate ganache to stick the chocolate curls all around the cake. I have to say, it looks almost as good as the photos I have in my wedding leaflets. I'm so carried away I tell Laurence I'll make the cake and save £300. His face glows positively pink with pride at my wife-ly baking skills – or is it delight at saving £300? A twinge of regret shoots through my tired neck almost before the words leave my mouth. Is it a premonition of the baking nightmare I've unleashed? He is so ridiculously pleased that I suppose I'm going to have to make it now, aren't I?

Friday 28th February

Despite headaches from the diet I make it through the day on eggs, bacon and other high fat foods that I don't normally touch. Yet when I meet Laurence for a relaxing spa session after work I can tell him I've lost 3lbs already this week. The price to pay is that I feel very odd, slightly sick and not very relaxed.

I manage to track down two bridesmaid books for Helen and Nicola. They are workbooks with room for photos and pictures that the girls can fill in before and after the day. I know it's the sort of memento I would have loved as a girl and I do want them both to have a truly memorable time. Later that evening Laurence rings the photographer John Mottershaw and I'm so thrilled to hear him chatting away about what we want. A few months ago he said he didn't want a photographer at all. Now we are just waiting for a price list and I'm keeping my fingers crossed that this month we have both made some real progress towards our wedding.

TRUSS ME – I'M A BRIDE

Monday 3rd March

After work Laurence and I set off for our appointment to view the village hall. It is only the second time we have actually been inside and I am quite relieved when Jill, the church Verger, leaves us alone to poke around. I take measurements for Lorraine's designs, while Laurence takes photographs as an aide memoir. I also begin an inventory of items that come with the hall that includes: 16 trestle tables, gold and burgundy crockery, 6 oak display panels, tea urn, 1 fridge, 1 freezer, 2 cookers and 12 old-fashioned wooden garden chairs.

A Place For Us

Venues

When transforming a venue, whether a barn, borrowed home or public venue, prepare a file with all relevant details:

- Measurements of main rooms, stage and external areas.
- Phone locations and telephone numbers.
- Keys and security systems.
- Numbers of loos and basins.
- Lighting, heating, sockets and PA systems.
- Licence regulations for entertainment and alcohol.

- Emergency exits, fire extinguishers and fire blankets.
- Any catering or cleaning equipment.
- Clarify what can be altered and what must be left alone.

Unfortunately, the cutlery and glasses are a jumble of styles and the majority of seats are plastic bucket style. An even bigger negative is Jill's news that the proposed lottery bid to get the hall repainted and extended has not been successful. We had very much been hoping for new French doors leading from the main hall out to the lawn and new disabled access and loos. This is disappointing, as even in the six months since we booked it, the hall is looking more careworn and paint-chipped. My sister is going to have to be very clever with that muslin swagging or some other designer's trick.

Outside on the lawn I close my eyes for a moment and imagine our guests milling around in the sunshine. It feels almost impossible to believe that we will transform this place. There's still so much work to do...

Wednesday 5th March

On cue our photographer's price list arrives and it looks reasonable with a very basic package starting at about £400. I've been so busy with work that by early evening I decide I deserve some R'n'R. I have a blissful hour at Borders bookshop leafing through wedding magazines, recipe books and honeymoon guides buried deep in a squidgy leather sofa. Eventually I buy a thick bridal magazine and a relaxation tape.

Sadly, a dreamy honeymoon for £500 seems unlikely. All the guides assume you have at least £3,000 to jet off to some private

beach resort so my only hope lies in the holiday competition details I've jotted down. Still, I suppose we could be very happy with a luxurious country house hotel weekend in the Lake District.

GETTING AWAY FROM IT ALL

HONEYMOONS

- The average spend on a honeymoon is £2,828.
- Many cash strapped couples are tempted to ask for cash gifts for a honeymoon instead of material gifts. In practice, close family members may open their wallets but relatives and friends may be offended by requests to pay for your flight upgrade or massage on the beach.
- The honeymoon ideal of an unforgettable trip means it's usual to opt for a few days of high luxury rather than two weeks of the usual holiday fare. On the other hand, if you are as stressed as most working couples, you may need to collapse somewhere peaceful for a proper holiday.
- Don't forget vaccinations and malaria tablet schedules, however busy you are.

Up to £500

- Consider a house swap (Intervac or Homelink) or beg a visit to a friend's house abroad.
- Rent a remote country cottage (from £250 per week) to get miles away from the crowds.
- With Eurostar prices from around £60 per person return, consider small romantic hotels in Bruges or Paris.

Up to £1,500

- The cheap flights networks can easily get you to some of

Europe's great cities. Search online for good rates at romantic hotels in Nice, St Petersburg, Vienna or Venice.
- Buy a package to a boutique hotel on the Med for upgraded quality and near-guaranteed sun.
- Canny shopping could buy you the long haul delights of South Africa, Thailand or Sri Lanka.

Over £1,500
- Of course you will be tempted to opt for an all inclusive beach holiday, but why jostle with other honeymooners?
- Go and see something truly unforgettable: the Northern Lights, Mount Kilimanjaro, Angkor Wat or Ayer's Rock. Stretch your budget by buying discount flights, staying at a top hotel for the first night and then using the Rough Guide.
- Do something unforgettable: stay on a vineyard or at a riding school; learn to sail or cook or surf together.
- Decide to do at least one thing together that requires a little courage (and no, I don't mean advanced bedroom gymnastics). Try a scuba lesson, learn salsa, climb that mountain or pony trek across the desert. Doing brave new things together is one of the best habits to come back from a honeymoon with.

TIP: *If you are very short of time and want a package, delegate your whole budget to a travel agent. They can also ensure you get any honeymoon freebies like extra nights and upgrades.*

Later, I try the relaxation tape. It is weirdly slow and sounds like an intermittent broadcast from an alien submarine. I lie down as instructed and next thing I know I'm floating off in a sky of golden clouds (or so I'm told by the droning electro-voice) and then it's all a blur. A success, then.

THURSDAY 6TH MARCH

After a hectic visit to a hospital assessing student projects I do a rash thing. I take a stroll for some air and walk straight into a high street bridal shop. Maybe it was the big red signs shouting 'Sale' across the windows, or my newly baggy trousers, but in one thoughtless moment I marched straight in and dived towards the 'Sale' rail.

DRESS FOR SUCCESS

THE GOWN

- It is unlikely you will have shopped for anything comparable to a wedding dress – in its complexity and individuality of fit.
- The traditional advice to start looking early makes good sense. Far more than conventional clothes, many dresses need to be seen on to appreciate their styling, design and impact on your figure.
- Think carefully about whom to take with you. If you think your family might bully you into a poor choice, go alone. If you think assistants will bully you, take a strong minded supporter.
- Bridal shops are notorious for trying to sell a complete package. Apparent savings on a wedding dress will soon be spent on the 'perfect' headdress and shoes – for you *and* the team of bridesmaids…

Cheap is the word. One hundred pounds, £200, £300. The rail sags with a variety of careworn dresses that nevertheless look incredible bargains.

A dark and wrinkled little lady zooms over.

"And what is it you're looking for," she asks in an Irish brogue that speaks of years of dressing girls in white – from confirmation frocks to wedding gowns to, I fear, laying them out in their final lacy shrouds.

Flummoxed as usual, I babble on about short sleeves and little jackets. I've developed a bit of a thing recently about flab on my upper arms.

"Ooh, you'd be what – a size 12, then?"

Blimey, the diet must be showing. "Oh, I don't think so." I shake my head apologetically. "Fourteen, perhaps?" I've actually got a 16 in my hands.

She appraises me in my slimming black trouser suit and purses her mouth as if I've just committed some venal sin. Just you wait, I think. Wedding dresses are cut for 18 year olds. They make no allowances for spreading waists or bosoms that bulge over bras. The more I think of it, this is strange given that the average age of the first time bride is currently 31.

"You just get behind that curtain and get down to your undies," the assistant commands. Why on earth didn't I put on some half decent underwear today? I'm wearing a black lace bra and beige nylon bloomers.

I stand in a peach coloured tent, sucking in my tum and thinking about all the midget virgins that she normally dresses, in their little trainer bras and thongs.

"Now just put these on."

She passes me a pair of grubby white platform heels circa glam rockers The Sweet in their 'Blockbuster' days. No way, I want to protest. But I dutifully squeeze my feet into them and, lo and behold, the mirror records my increase in height and flattering pelvic tilt. I look about 50% better already.

I try on dresses and the experience is, shall we say, intimate. This assistant may be wizened and unassuming but she has the strength of a cowgirl trussing up a prize steer. As predicted, the size 14 gapes over my ample bosom. No problem. She gets out a piece of string and somehow laces me into it.

"We can let it out a bit there, to fit just perfect," she announces. Sure, the front looks okay but I look like a bursting parcel from the back. This is distinctly off-putting and I think she realises I'm not going to be a pushover. I take a deep breath.

"I'd like to try the16." Wordlessly pursing those thin lips, she fetches it.

"Of course, the way they're all cut now, they're a size smaller in reality."

I nod in submission. After all, she's fully dressed and I'm flobbing around in a pair of knickers I now wish I'd thrown out in the 1970s.

This dress fits perfectly. The zip purrs up my spine and the bodice embraces rather than tortures my waist. Even the décolletage isn't low enough to risk indecent exposure at the altar steps. There are little cupped sleeves that cover my arms. It is the first wedding dress I have tried on that fits me perfectly and I naturally go all gooey eyed – for a few minutes, anyway.

Such is my infatuation with the snug fit that I even follow the assistant's prompting to admire myself in the huge full length mirrors out on the shop floor. As I totter forwards on my platform heels an unfamiliar sensation surrounds my legs. I have been so focussed on the miraculously fitting bodice that I haven't paid much attention to the generous skirts. Looking in the mirror, there's just a whiff of Bo-Beep about the dress. Remember that one dress Andie McDowell tries on for Hugh Grant in Four Weddings? The one that's so twee that even he, who is crazy about her, can't avoid a little wince of pain as she sashays forward, bonnet on head and crook in hand? That's what this dress is like. The skirt surges with a life of its own around my legs. It should feel romantic but it feels weirdly unstable, like some sort of giant puffball on the rampage. The mirror says it all. Marie Antoinette on a bad day down at the Model Farm. No way.

And all through this, my assistant is giving a little commentary. "Ooh that's lovely, perfect fit, you won't find anything better, only £250, made for you, you could look forever and never find better," and on and on.

"I'll have to think about it." I swirl around and my skirt catches up with me about a minute later. It's too big, noisy, intrusive and – the sort of thing someone who thinks starving masses should eat cake would wear. Non, non, non!

"You really should take it now." My little lady is as sharp as her sheaf of pins. "You won't find a better fit."

I look again. Could she be right?

"I don't know," I falter.

"Just a £50 deposit and it's yours."

Silence. What can I say?

"I'd like to look around, first."

"But I've told you, you won't find anything better. Especially not at this price. You will *never* find anything better."

Suddenly I'm desperate to take the dress off. But such are wedding dresses, you cannot remove them unassisted. I stand my ground and meet her eye. I can be stubborn, too.

"I need to talk to my mother about it. She's paying. I'll get back in touch."

She points at the phone. "Give her a ring now."

I feel like I'm that trussed up steer again, only this time I can smell the coals on the barbie.

"She's out," I shoot back. "I'll speak to her tonight. But she would have to see it."

"So when can she come in?"

"Oh, *I* don't know."

Silence. Just lie, I think. Just get out of here. I sigh loudly.

"Maybe Saturday."

"Well, I'll put your name on it," my tormentor accedes. "And keep it on one side for you."

Finally, finally, she undoes the laces and I can clamber out of the dress, which deflates like a parachute on the showroom floor.

I go through the empty motions of giving my contact details, which are pinned onto the dress as it's taken off to some holding area.

"Now you must come in to pay your deposit by Saturday," the woman instructs.

I pick up a card with the shop's phone number and write CANCEL on the back as soon as I get outside. I can still feel the imprints of the trussing on my back and the haunting rustle of ballooning skirts around my legs as I hurry back to my car. Oh, to wear trousers again and not have to sashay along the pavement with 10 yards of stiffened taffeta repelling passers-by. It feels like a very narrow escape indeed.

Sunday 9th March

After church this morning, Laurence takes some beautiful photographs of the stained glass in the Grosvenor Chapel. The images are of the Four Evangelists and when he gets home he begins to edit the images for our invitations. It's such a relief to feel he's interested.

Later, we call into the shops and I see the Denby Greenwich range of pottery on display at Allders. Calling Laurence over, we both like the glass goblets and sturdy crockery. I write down details on our 'running list' of wedding presents when I get home but am rather concerned at the prices. I don't want people thinking we are greedy – and yet already family and friends are constantly asking for a copy of our wedding list.

Monday 10th March

As I'm working at the computer I also rattle off a few confirmation letters. Having slept on the Florist issue, I've decided to book Sue. She offers the best prices, seems very used to setting up wedding flowers and is reasonably local. I also send a written acceptance of the furniture quote, which had to be confirmed within 30 days.

Getting Organised

Putting It In Writing

- Writing to all your suppliers is the best way to prevent misunderstandings over the contract between you.
- If you verbally amend the contract write again, confirming any changes.

- Print off a 'File Copy' of every letter for yourself as a crucial record to be kept safely in your folder.
- In letters remember to include:
  - your name and address and contact details including mobile phone number
  - your new address if moving home
  - today's date and the wedding date
  - reference or order number if given
  - your wedding or delivery venue and address
  - any delivery or set up arrangements
  - an exact description of the goods or services
  - the price you have agreed (with VAT if required)

TIP: *Email can go astray or bounce. Either ask for a confirmation email or print off and send a copy by snail mail.*

TUESDAY 25TH MARCH

The month has been flying by, with my planned goals for work and wedding prep falling by the wayside. One problem has been the clash with our home improvements. Keith has been installing our bathroom and I know I couldn't wish for a friendlier, more considerate or neater person around the house but…well, there's the noise, for example, of our old bath, sink and loo being ripped out of the floorboards. And naturally, Keith occasionally needs a second opinion on the shower rail or the tile trim or how the cabinets should sit. Then we stop and have a cup of tea or we get chatting or I have to flee the house to get away from the drilling just the other side of the wall from my computer screen.

The first victim of all this is concentration – and with concentration goes The Plan and then The Diet. I've waited whole days to ring suppliers because I'm apprehensive that half way through a difficult conversation the drill will start up and I won't hear a thing. As for the diet, it must be the corned beef sandwiches I make for Keith or just having someone around in the kitchen. Today, after weighing myself on the gym scales (which must be wrong) I'm back on the diet with a vengeance. Oh, but the bathroom is a gorgeous blue and white extravaganza and when I finally take my first luxurious bath and shower I'm delighted we've gone ahead with it.

Sunday 30th March

I've had a strange phone call relating to one of the competitions I recently entered in 'Lancashire and Cheshire Bride'. The prize is £1,500 worth of 'Dreamaker Wedding Organisation' and as an avid comper I simply saw the words 'wedding' and 'win' and entered it without thinking. The result is a phone call to say that we are one of the final three couples competing for the prize and can I please arrange to meet the Wedding Organiser and tell her all about our wedding.

Getting the magazine out I find the article:
To win this fantastic prize tell us in no more than 35 words why you would like to win the services of a wedding co-ordinator...'

I had replied with this awful ditty:
'Fixed our date but panic's chronic, we dream of flowers and choirs symphonic but plans and sketches look moronic – Dreamaker sounds the perfect tonic!'

Oh dear! It's one thing to throw something like that into the post and another to actually go and talk about it to a real life Wedding Organiser. How truthful will I have to be? Choirs symphonic? It sounds like I dream of the Mormon Tabernacle Choir invading our village church. Yuk. I tell Laurence, cringing with embarrassment. He gives me one of those withering 'What have you got us into now?' looks.

"Well, we could do with the £1,500. Can't they give us the cash?"

"I don't think so." I know so. No cash equivalent. "Maybe she could organise the flowers? Or the clothes or something." I'm trying to be simultaneously vague and optimistic.

"But flowers and clothes don't cost that much. Do they?" He really does look worried now. "I'm not going to have to do anything embarrassing am I? My family are going to be there." He's imagining the worst. Grotesque sentimentality – being asked to karaoke sing Abba's 'I Do I Do I Do' in the middle of the church service, or a dominatrix type Wedding Organiser bullying our guests into submission. Even worse, he's imagining elderly guests in tears on the sidelines, rejected from the photo shoot as insufficiently photogenic for 'Cheshire Bride'.

Suddenly he hardens. "If it means we have to do anything tasteless, we don't want the prize. Agreed?"

"Okay. But if we win we will have to be in the magazine."

"That's all right. We'll get free photography."

"So it's okay for me to meet her?" He nods, but gives me that 'Me Moses Lawgiver/You Daft Delilah' look. It means, 'Watch it, you. Don't push me too far.'

I spend the afternoon putting my case together for us being the winning couple. I decide that our Unique Selling Point sadly isn't us, but is Eccleston and its beautiful setting. I am certainly not hopeful of winning, but then again neither am I sure that winning a wedding organiser is what we want anyway.

TO DO:

Try to make fundamental shift from superficial list-maniac to a more profound type person with inner karma based on fact that wedding is only one day of whole life, worse things happen at sea, could be dead or dying, etc. Maybe take up meditation. Or voluntary work. Feeling panicked already by prospect of time consuming task of becoming a better person. Maybe will be better person ***after*** *wedding when have more time…*

More urgent – *lose pounds that have piled on over last week. Will new fat come off faster, ie not as cosily settled as old fat?*

Even More Urgent – *must steel myself to meet Wedding Organiser. She must be expecting very weird 'Some Mothers Do 'Ave 'Em' type couple based on ditty. Moronic? Chronic? Or maybe it's true? Maybe ditty contains deep profound insights…*

And do I really want to be media bride plastered all over mags? Can imagine seeing self featured bursting out of dress in list of Worst Wedding Horrors. Must check I can pull out of Wedding Competition. Did I sign entry form? Is it a contract? Do not want additional stress of legal fees draining already cringeworthy budget.

Most urgent of all – *must calm down. Take deep breaths. Take charge. Take bath in beautiful bathroom. Take more primrose oil. Take it all on, for better or worse…*

THE ZIPPER FITS

TUESDAY 1ST APRIL

My nightmare about having nothing to wear for the wedding keeps returning, leaving me hyperventilating in the dark while Laurence snozzles peacefully beside me. This morning my nightmare took me as far as the church vestry where all I could find to wear was a tatty maribou stole. And yes, I mean *all*. The thought of getting arrested for indecent exposure on my wedding day holds no appeal at all, thank you. To make matters worse (and the exposure even more humiliating), after a brilliant start with the Clarke diet, the cruel facts are that I've only lost 7lbs since my heavyweight weigh-in after Christmas. And that's 2lb heavier than two weeks ago.

SATURDAY 5TH APRIL

We spend the evening working on our invitations. Laurence has taken some beautiful photographs of Pre-Raphaelite figures from church windows and chosen two to represent ourselves. Using a computer package, he has subtly superimposed the word 'Laurence' across one figure and 'Laura' on the other. These have been printed on a cream watercolour weight outer card while the inner sheet is plain paper printed with black ink. The invitations look very beautiful and delicate, and most importantly, are unique to us.

Our guest numbers have recently been growing and I've had to tell Laurence that 70 is our absolute maximum. Food and drink alone will be at least £30 per head.

INVITATIONS

CUTTING THE NUMBERS

- The cost of your wedding is largely determined by the number of guests. Play around with the cost per guest. Decide the maximum number of guests (including any quotas for parents' friends vs your own guests) and stick firm.
- Using address books, draft a guest list of Definites and Possibles and then ask yourself: Has this person been in touch over the last 12 months? If not, don't feel too guilty about rejecting them.
- If the numbers are still too big, consider culling whole groups (everyone from the football team) rather than pulling out individuals.
- The serious spending occurs when guests sit down for a wedding meal, so shift whole groups onto an evening list.

We have named ourselves as the hosts and also decided to be informal and omit our surnames. As Laurence dislikes the word *reception* with its connotations of endless speeches, we've agreed on the phrase *Celebration Meal.*

LAURENCE & LAURA
WOULD LIKE YOU TO JOIN THEM TO CELEBRATE
THEIR MARRIAGE AT
THE CHURCH OF ST MARY THE VIRGIN, ECCLESTON, CHESTER,
ON SATURDAY 30TH AUGUST 2003
AT 3 PM
AND AFTERWARDS AT A CELEBRATION DINNER
AND COUNTRY CEILIDH
AT ECCLESTON VILLAGE HALL

We've also produced a brief Evening Invitation and a reply card so people don't have to buy acceptance cards.

MAKING AND BREAKING THE RULES

INVITATIONS

Traditionally, invitations are sent from the bride's parents as hosts: 'Mr and Mrs Proud Parents request the pleasure of your company…' Modern wording tends towards a more casual approach (so long as the chief payers are not offended):

- Jointly from the families of the couple if everyone is chipping in together.
- From the couple with a casual intro: 'The rumours are true…'
- From your own children as 'hosts' if you have any.
- Wedding etiquette suggests invites go out 6 weeks before the wedding – a sure fire method of halving your guest list due to prior engagements. Three to six months is more practical.
- Send out 'Save the Date' cards if your invites aren't ready.

- Only state the dress code if it's Black Tie or a theme like '1920s'.
- Ask for dietary requirements with your RSVPs.

Card, envelopes and inks to make your own: £10-50
Standard printed invitations for 100 guests: £200-300
Handcrafted invitations using feathers, beads or fabric: up to £5 each

SUNDAY 6TH APRIL

A new couple, Ben and Esther, have moved into the house next door, and today we finally manage to arrange a time to get together and chat. Almost the first thing I find out over coffee is that they were married at Eccleston last July. It seems an incredible coincidence and I bombard them with questions which they, being relatively newlywed, seem happy to answer.

Their wedding arrangements differed from ours in some crucial ways. Firstly, they went for a very big wedding complete with 'pink' theme featuring three grown-up bridesmaids in elegant pink dresses and two best men and three groomsmen in pink cravats. After their wedding at Eccleston they held a reception at Soughton Hall, a stunning country house hotel on the Welsh border where many of the guests stayed overnight, allowing for late night revelry.

What we do have in common is that Ben and Esther also exercised their creative brain cells and did some hard work. They made their own invitations using metallic paints and even collected pebbles and hand-painted them in pink as place markers. The impression I get is of a lavish and lovely affair.

So it was all perfectly relaxed, right up to the wedding eve?

"I couldn't sleep, I was shaking so much," groans Esther.

Ben laughs. "It was fantastic. But we'd never go through it again..."

FRIDAY 11TH APRIL

Today it's my appointment with Alison, the wedding organiser. She wants to meet at Boundary Mill, a vast 'seconds' outlet in Colne. I meet her in the cafe and I can see her eyeing me up shrewdly – am I magazine material or a true wedding duffer? Sadly, it must be the latter. I pick up from her body language that we won't be the winning couple and decide that it's much more interesting to get a professional's view of wedding planning than to win a prize we really don't want. After more than an hour of intensive interviewing (mostly me of her) I have jotted down pages of tips gleaned from the hundreds of weddings she has been involved with.

GETTING ORGANISED

TIPS FROM A WEDDING ORGANISER

- A theme is important, especially for visual impact. Some of the best are carried through the whole day, like butterflies or ladybirds. At one wedding she used trails of little ladybirds across tables, on invitations and on dresses.
- For catering serve something different. Mini Magnum ice creams served from trays look lovely, or strawberries dipped in chocolate.
- Avoid anything with fresh cream in the summer. Croquembouche (a tower of cream filled profiteroles) goes sour in the sun.

- Don't try to overentertain. One couple wanted a troubadour, a magician, and a loud band with a singer – and people were covering up their ears. Often relatives have travelled a fair distance and want some time to chat and mingle quietly.
- Get taxis ordered as a signal that it's time to go home. Especially if you're hiring a private hall, guests may only think about going home once the band finishes. After waiting as much as an hour for a taxi, they'll forget the wonderful time they had and just remember sitting around getting fed up.

TIP: *Beware the contracts in some bridal shops. One client had such a hard sell that she signed her name just to get away. When she rang to cancel they refused. The dress cost thousands and despite solicitor's letters, they had such a tightly worded contract that she had to pay for it – even though she never even wore it.*

Finally, I ask for some feedback on our plans. The caterers have a good reputation, she confirms. The venue also looks good, but she warns me that it will be a lot of work to do it ourselves. Finally, she tells me she can't believe I haven't got my dress yet. She warns that if I don't get it ordered now I risk having to pay a £100 express charge if I need it within six weeks of the wedding.

Simultaneously relieved at a bona fide expert not throwing her hands up in horror at my wedding plans, and yet also panicked by her remarks about dresses, I rush off to a couple of bridal shops. Nothing appeals or they are way too expensive. The result is this feeling of strangled panic, just like my nightmare scenario.

SATURDAY 12TH APRIL

Today I'm off to a Society of Authors' meeting but I'm so early that I drive into Lancaster city centre for a quick look around. Miraculously, I see a branch of Pronuptia with an empty parking space outside. Still with 40 minutes to kill, I pull up and the shop is blissfully empty. I try on a couple of straight skirts with bodices. The first one I try on is gorgeous, gorgeous, gorgeous. It is made of white satin with a square neck and long train. I feel sure it could be The One and feel almost speechless with surprise and relief. Under pressure from the assistant, I nevertheless make my excuses and get away to my meeting. Lancaster is too far from Chester to realistically call in for fittings or even to pick it up.

MONDAY 14TH APRIL

All weekend I've been childishly excited about the dress and spent guilty sessions poring over my bridal mags until I found it. I ring my mum and warn her that it's £540. She's happy to buy it, but I can't relax about it.

I wake up determined to sort out my dress – today. Putting my work guiltily to one side I get out the Yellow Pages and make a list of every bridal shop I've not yet visited in the area. I want to satisfy myself that I've not missed any alternative bargains. The weather is gloriously sunny as I set off with a list of shops and an A–Z road map beside me. The first place I try to find is down tiny country lanes and just looks like someone's house. Maybe they actually do sell dresses from home but I strongly suggest they get a sign made if they want any business. I choose not to ring the doorbell and ask "Do you sell wedding dresses?" like some mad woman. Annoyed, I drive on.

In Wrexham I find my second shop. This one is in a row of terraced houses and my first impression is that it's cheap. Too cheap. There are dresses hanging on rails for £100. I try one on and realise quickly that you get what you pay for. These dresses are unlined and poorly made. I make my apologies and leave.

Parking in town I hope it will be third time lucky. Annie's Brides is relaxed and homely, with a seamstress busy pressing gowns in the corner and Annie herself eager to help. For such a small shop there are a number of possible dresses and I start trying them on. Now, at last, as reward for all those excruciating trying-on sessions, I can describe to Annie exactly what I'm looking for. A tight bodice, a straight skirt, something flattering without too much flesh on show.

"I've just got one back from hire." She's listening hard and thinking even harder. "It's absolutely gorgeous. Only it's in a bit of a state."

"Can I see it?" I'm standing behind the voluminous curtains, urging her on.

"Do you mind if it's a bit dirty? It only came back last night."

"Honestly. I don't mind." I nearly push her out of the changing room.

This time I'm well prepared for stripping off. I'm wearing an all-in-one white lace teddy affair that pushes me up and pulls me in, in all the right places. I'm so intent on my mission that I feel like barging into the back rooms with Annie, in search of this mysteriously filthy dress.

At first glance, it's love. Champagne satin – not white. If there was a problem with the Pronuptia dress it was *too* bright white. This is softly creamy, peachy, ivory. Yet the embroidery, beading and crystals on the bodice are sparkling white. I pull on the skirt

and Annie says, "We'll probably have to alter it. The last bride had it taken in."

No. It fits like a dream. Skims my hips, reaches the tips of my shoes and hooks up perfectly. The bodice is divine and to my utter relief isn't too low and zips up as tight and snug as if it had been made for me. The train is a long oval of embroidered and beaded fabric that hooks onto the skirt waist. It looks fabulous as it fish-tails behind me.

"You can wear the train for the ceremony and then unhook it later." Annie is tying a set of criss-cross laces up the smooth back of the bodice. I parade up and down the floor and find I can walk well and the boning of the bodice makes me hold my back ram-rod straight. It looks better than I had ever imagined a dress looking. The dress is by Veromia, an off-the-peg brand in the £600-£1,000 range. The embroidery is almost baroque in its curlicues and crystals and the boning makes my middle look like an hour-glass. I don't ever want to take it off.

"It's to hire?" I ask. "Is it free on 30th August?"

I hold my breath as she goes off to consult her book.

"Yes. You can come in for a fitting at the beginning of August just in case there need to be any adjustments."

"And how much is it?"

"You pay for a week's hire. It's £250. That includes any alterations."

"And it will be cleaned and tidied up?" It is filthy. The last bride certainly had a good time in it – the seam at the back of the skirt is split and there are marks I don't want to inspect too closely on the satin. Annie assures me that it will be spotless and pressed, and also that no one else will be able to hire it so it won't get damaged or disappear. I'll take it, I assure her. I'll be back with my mum on the following Saturday to pay our deposit. I'm walking well above the cobbles as I leave, so thrilled and excited that I've got my dress. And even better is the fact that it's hired. There will be no mouldering, wine stained rags in my attic, thanks.

Dress For Success

Hiring Outfits

Hiring men's outfits is easy. Hiring women's outfits may take a bit more detective work:

- Shops that hire do so as a sideline to selling gowns. They tend not to advertise as they would rather you buy outright. Check out Yellow Pages or local newspaper wedding directories.
- The trend is moving away from hiring, partly due to a proportion of brides who either ruin the dress or fail to return it.
- Alternatively, cut out the middleman and borrow a dress from a recent bride. After all, it's only been worn once.

Why choose to hire?

- Cost – expect to pay about one-third of the dress price as new, including cleaning and alterations
- No bulky storage, specialist laundering or packing boxes
- No post-wedding tears over the inevitable stains and rips
- None of the hassle of selling your Cinderella gown after the Ball

And why not?

- Limited time (about a week) to match underwear and accessories. (Get a swatch and take a photo.)

- Return of the outfit needs to be delegated if you're going straight off on your honeymoon.
- You've lost your life's chance to have one, fabulous, fairy-tale dress created uniquely for you.
- *Local high street dress hire:*
  Wedding gowns: from £150
  Bridesmaids: from £50

EASTER MONDAY 21ST APRIL

It is my mum's last day over with us and we have had a lovely time – Laurence's parents came over for Easter lunch, we have visited Powis castle and my dress has been approved of, admired and paid for. While Mum's been with us, I've been trying to understand her attitude to the wedding. She has been wonderfully generous but she does shake her head sometimes and ask why we want all this fuss. Looking at pictures of her own wedding day does give me some insight – she was a beautiful Dutch girl visiting England just after the war when she met Dad. They had a minimal wedding at a London register office like many couples at that time.

And then, of course, there is my parents' divorce. One of the reasons we're opting out of a traditional top table is so we can seat everyone without obvious precedence at a round table. After checking out how both my parents feel, we've jumbled up Keith, my mum, Chris, Laurence's parents, Dad, his partner Olivia, Jonathan and ourselves on our own circular wedding table.

Then there's Mum's outfit. "What I'd like to wear is my old black trouser suit," she tells me. "Please, Mum," I beg. "Don't wear black on my wedding day."

I know Mum adores Laurence and is so thrilled that I'm getting married, so that's the important thing. I suppose that not all mums go into ecstasies about chiffon and pearl studded rosebuds. Thankfully, we haven't encountered too many of the heart-rending family conflicts so many couples face…

Family Foibles

They're Driving Me Crazy!

It's supposed to be bliss but instead it's a battlefield. There's something about a wedding that unearths deep emotions – both loving and less positive…

'Help! My parents are taking over. I know they are contributing cash but my mum can recite whole paragraphs of 1950s wedding etiquette.'

- Crucially, you must get together with your partner and agree on all the major issues. Then explain your shared vision of the wedding to your parents.
- Allocate cash contributions to particular budget items and delegate some of those items directly to your parents to organise. Try to keep them busy and, most importantly, help them feel appreciated.
- If they won't leave your plans alone, firmly tell them you love having their support, but you and your partner want to grow together as a working team.

'My elder sister is sulking because she wants to be chief bridesmaid but I want my best friend. I'm the bride so I'm right, aren't I?'

For sister you could substitute dad and step-dad vying to be giver away, or old friend and brother competing to be best man. Suddenly people are realising just how much (or how little) you value them. Of course that's not your intention, but it's what recipients can feel. If you are destroying a long cher-

ished dream, ask yourself if it's worth it:

- Compromise. Can you have both? Dad can give you away, step-dad can give a special reading. Have two chief bridesmaids – just carve up the tasks between them.
- Invent new roles like guest book guardian, or swap gender roles to create a best woman or chief groomsman.
- If it all gets too much, insist that just you and your partner will carry out any contentious tasks yourselves, rather than wasting time squabbling.

'I can't believe people's strange behaviour. Are they actually jealous?'
Envy of the bride-to-be is common and may surface as a lack of co-operation or catty remarks about silly weddings. More seriously, you may unwittingly invite someone who finds the whole issue of you being the centre of loving attention emotionally intolerable:

- With the support of your partner and other allies, let all but serious attacks flow over you.
- If a divorced mum or lovelorn friend is having a hard time coping, do explain how much you care for them and need their support. Tell them you've noticed they aren't enjoying the wedding experience and give them an opportunity to opt out of any stressful roles.
- If someone is bitchy to your face, keep asking them politely to explain their remarks and why on earth they think that way.
- If someone gets abusive or makes a play for the groom, you have the perfect grounds to ban them from your wedding.

'One guest has told me they won't attend my wedding if another guest

they loathe does. How do I choose?'

It could be a long standing family feud or your own divorced mum and dad who refuse to attend together:

- In the case of B-list guests who threaten you with this unreasonable behaviour, consider them as having uninvited themselves. Explain that your wedding is a symbol of love and co-operation and if they can't enter into the spirit for one special day that's a terrible shame – for them, not you.
- If, sadly, the two enemies are close family members, both of whom you desperately want to be present, appeal to their better natures. Tell them you need them both to support you on this special day.
- Clarify that rather than hurting each other, they are torturing you. Think of clever ways to keep both parties separate throughout the day and propose this as a peace offering.
- Explain that if they don't attend, you will be forced to tell everyone the reason and how hurt you will feel. Hopefully, like most blackmailers, the threat of a public airing of their bad behaviour will make them think again.

CONGRATULATIONS!

SATURDAY 3RD MAY

10AM: Just as I feel things are moving forward I get a sharp jolt. My bridesmaid Helen's mum phones me in a flap:

"We've just been to Meadow Hall to get the bridesmaid's dress. And they don't have it in Age 7–8. Or even Age 9–10."

As soon as I had chosen my own dress last month, I emailed both bridesmaids' mums asking them to pick up the Pierce Fonda Designer at Debenhams bridesmaids dresses in ivory. Shortly afterwards, Nicola's mum picked up her dress at Manchester and I'd posted off a very modest £55 cheque to cover the cost.

"And I asked the girl to ring round," Hilary continues, "and they've sold out through the whole country!"

"Let's not panic," I say, trying to slow Hilary down. "I'm sure there are lots in that style in Chester. I'll go and have a look. Now."

I drive into Chester. No luck. Even worse, when the assistant interrogates the database there are a few false cyber sightings of the dress (in Ipswich of all places) but when she rings they don't exist.

Smart Shopping

Seasons And Sales

- The more complete sets of anything you need (bridesmaid's frocks, candelabras, purple cravats) the sooner you need to buy them.
- Children grow at an alarming rate. It's sensible to buy the next size up and shorten if necessary.
- Co-ordinating the hire or purchase of a large numbers of attendants' outfits is time consuming and tedious. Delegate to a determined mum, chief bridesmaid or best man.
- If you are giving attendants choices of fabric or dress style, set an early cut-off date after which malingerers will have to fall in with your decision.

12 NOON: I remember Angela's comment that there were lots of dresses left at the Trafford Centre. I clock up another 50 miles in the car, dash to the rail and – no. Only toddler sizes left. Again I ask the assistant to check the database.

"I'm sorry, it's coming up with nothing across the whole country," she commiserates. I walk away, feeling devastated. But I don't know where to go, so on an impulse I turn back to her and ask, "Is the database always accurate? I really am desperate for this dress."

"Well, there are ways of searching more accurately," she confides. "I really shouldn't do this but someone once showed me how to do it." She brushes in a few more keystrokes. "Ah, here's something. Manchester. Age 9-10. Ivory Pierce Fonda. Only it's shop soiled."

I want to snaffle the girl's hand off with joy. "Can you ring them? Can they keep it? I'll go straight over."

It's another hour of frantic inner city driving before I get there. Until I see and touch this dress I won't believe it.

3PM: The dress is brought down from a stock room. It's the right style and size and although grubby is undamaged. I could kiss the girl who presents it to me.

"I'll have to give you a discount," she says, shaking her head at the dirty hem and ribbons.

"Okay,'"I agree, not betraying that I would probably have paid double the price just to get my mitts on it.

5PM: I take the dress home and hang it up in our bedroom like a victory flag. At Age 9-10 it's almost adult size – an ivory satin bodice with fabric roses around the high waist and a long sash at the back. The skirt falls away in gauzy petals over an underskirt of creamy fabric. Laurence thinks it's lovely, especially when I tell him the price. "If that's £45, why are wedding dresses so expensive?"

"Search me," I say, flopping down on the bed. "Just don't search the Debenhams database," I groan.

SATURDAY 10TH MAY

We set off to visit Laurence's friends in Sheffield today and my reward for last week's runaround is seeing Helen model her dress. It looks so pretty on her and I'm so thrilled now our plans are taking some kind of shape. Next, we visit John, the photographer in Grindleford, and have a good rifle through his albums and samples of pictures. We both like a black Ravello album with prints mounted on plain black pages. Finally, we agree to 38 10 x 8 pictures and a variety of 'reportage' snaps for a total price of £685. Telling him that I'll email him a list of suggested shots, we take our leave.

Pleasures To Treasure

Photography

- Think hard before letting an enthusiastic guest take your photographs. Your photos are the one truly vivid memento of your wedding.
- Look for technical skills in composition and lighting and the ability to catch a relaxed and natural pose.
- Ask to see a range of weddings, not just a publicity album taken of the truly photogenic in perfect light conditions. How does the photographer cope with rain? Harsh sunlight? Dark interiors?
- A wedding photographer needs to direct guests without irritating or bullying. What strategies will they use to manage 100+ people?
- 'Reportage' photography captures unposed moments as they happen but may omit unique shots you didn't realise you wanted until you review your album – such as a portrait of you, your mum and grandma.
- It's your job to give your photographer a storyboard of images in advance. On the day, you may be incapable of knowing what you want.
- Special effects include black and white, soft focus, sepia and dramatic hand tints. Go easy on these and opt for a majority of classic portraits that won't date too quickly.

Local photographer – classic shots in traditional album: £500-900
Storybook album with a few special effects: about £1,000-1,400

> *Reportage album including engagement shoot, 'behind the scenes', aerial and fun shots: £1,500-2,500*

After a quick pub meal we find the venue where a recommended Ceilidh band is playing. I'm keen to clock up as many bookings as possible so I chat away to the bearded dance caller about our wedding. Laurence stays silent and then gives his verdict.

"I reckon that guy's stoned," he says. "Just watch."

From the sidelines I take his point. The whole atmosphere is rather too hand knitted jerkins and pudding basin haircuts. Our friend the caller is standing ramrod straight, only his mouth moving, like some empty eyed hick who's had too much moonshine. Then he suddenly throws a fit, bullying some kids who get their footwork in the wrong order. Not a good omen…

SUNDAY 11TH MAY

Time for a post mortem on our Sheffield trip. Laurence is pleased with the photos, although I note we've gone way over budget. I'm thrilled with the bridesmaid's dress, but after sleeping on it, neither of us are too keen on the band.

Laurence suggests we look for someone else and I do a massive search on the internet. I know that some good local bands are already booked for 30th August as it's a very popular Saturday night for all kinds of events. I do get one promising email back from an agency who tell us that Devil's Fire are free: a four piece band with fiddle, drums, guitar and bass. They can do a mixture of Ceilidh, popular and instrumental music and have good recommendations from audiences at weddings. The price is £530 and they'll send us a CD. What is happening to our budget?

In the evening, we finally get the last of our day invitations signed, sealed and stamped. It's a relief to slide them all into the post box and head home, knowing that although we are behind our original schedule, at least we have got them out three months in advance.

Saturday 17th May

We've been listening to the CD sent to us by Devil's Fire and it's foot tapping bluegrass stuff so we've decided to book them. The contract is excellent, pointing out exactly what we need to do (provide parking, a socket, small table, stage, and of course, fee). We also get a really exciting wedding acceptance today from Laurence's friends Al and Kate and daughter Leah. I've been dreading that many of our friends will decline so I'm thrilled they can come. It's wonderful to be getting acceptance cards back and I'm trying my best to file them and keep a running list of who is definitely coming along.

One thing I could have improved is our invitation paperwork. It has been amazingly difficult to get hold of some relatives' addresses and then we've made the foolish mistake of not keeping all addresses in one folder. Also, I've been sending different information out to different people at different stages by post and by email.

Getting Organised

Writing To Guests

- Keep a database (or simple list) of all names and addresses and print out or copy as required.
- Keep a ticklist of information sent (accommodation lists,

gift lists, maps) and information received (RSVPs, seating requests and gifts).

- Recent research has concluded that a guest can spend as much as £400 per head on outfit, gift, travel, overnight accommodation and meals. Be sensitive to what guests can afford.
- Guests will feel well cared for if you provide parking directions, sightseeing and hotel guides, taxi company details and extra information about the day such as meal times or crèche facilities.

WEDNESDAY 21ST MAY

Just as I'm leaving on my business trip, suitcase in hand and mind on the work ahead, the postman thrusts a padded envelope into my hand. There's a label stating 'Wedding and Home' on the front. Stationery samples, I wonder? Yet more bridal bumph? I almost dump it on the sideboard but curiosity makes me tear open the edge.

> *'Dear Laura,*
> *Congratulations! This letter is to confirm that you are the lucky winner of our Jamaica honeymoon competition. You have won a fabulous honeymoon at the Tryall Club, Montego Bay, Jamaica…'*

I can hardly read the details as so much adrenaline is hurtling round my system. Unbelievable! I have to sit down and reread the letter again and again. The competition was a simple postcard draw I vaguely remember entering a month or so ago. Finally, it sinks in. We've won our honeymoon! I leave Laurence a breathless message on his mobile, pack the envelope to study at leisure and beam all the way through the traffic.

Smart Shopping

Bridal Competitions

- Take advantage of the many promotions, prize draws and competitions organised by bridal magazines and fairs.
- Remember many competitors disqualify themselves by missing the closing date or not completing the entry form completely or correctly.
- If a slogan (tiebreaker) is required, be aware that around 85% of winning entries rhyme or contain a pun – eg *'Sugar-white beaches, waters blue – it's my dream 'aisle' to say 'I do…'*.
- Start early to increase your chances. Valuable 'Win A Complete Wedding Package' prizes are out of reach to many couples once reception deposits are paid.

TIP: *Cinemas and bars often have racks of free promotional postcards – invaluable and eye catching for free prize draws.*

THE SLOSH ACCOUNT

SUNDAY 1ST JUNE

It has been agony working away from home this last week but today I get home to Laurence – wonderful! At last we can talk about Jamaica and we're both singing the old 'Montego Bay' pop song like two barmy kids. I've had a look at the website and the Tryall Club looks gorgeous – big white villas, turquoise ocean, lush sugar plantation. A perfect honeymoon. And to my relief, I've had confirmation that they can fit us in from the Wednesday after the wedding. Just the flights to sort out now…

Laurence has cooked a delicious Turkey and Broccoli Gratin and his own special Irish banana cake. It's all so yummy that any thoughts of the diet disappear. I think about how lucky we are to be together and how well suited to each other's temperaments. Over dinner we chat about our wedding gift list and amazingly, Laurence is keen to come with me tomorrow and choose our items.

PLEASURES TO TREASURE

GIFT LISTS

The age old tradition of giving gifts to newlyweds means you will undoubtedly be bombarded with requests for gift ideas:

- Even if you already have everything in the world you could ever want, guests will appreciate some guidance about gifts to a charity or church fund. You can set up a building society account that anyone can pay into (just give them the account number) so they can contribute anonymously to a charity fund.
- Around 65% of couples set up a store list containing items they have chosen to suit their home. The main providers are: Marks and Spencer, John Lewis, Argos, Debenhams and Allders. You choose the items and they manage the list, delivery and optional gift wrapping.
- The advent of online wedding lists means you can track gift buying via your PC, change and add to the list and print off guest names ready for your thank you cards.
- Reportedly, four out of 10 couples now ask guests for a financial contribution, whether for a honeymoon, a house or to cover the wedding costs. Thinly disguised requests (gift vouchers, premium bonds or assigned accounts called *House Deposit* or *Church Flower Fund*) will be more acceptable to many relatives and friends than upfront requests for cash.

The total cost of items on an average wedding gift list is about £1,000-1,400

The average guest spends £30-40 on a wedding gift

The most popular items are wine goblets, dinner plates, champagne flutes, pillowcases and tablemats

And in case you are feeling guilty:

The Earl and Countess of Wessex reportedly had a £42,000 tea service on their list.

MONDAY 2ND JUNE

It feels wonderfully wicked to take Monday off and go into Chester together. I've done a quick review of the main wedding list providers and plumped for Browns of Chester aka Debenhams. We meet one of the wedding gift organisers who tells us that Monday morning is an excellent time to make a list as on late nights and weekends there are so many couples that they run out of scanners. As a first step today we wander around with a clipboard. After Laurence has interrogated the assistants about durability and replaceability, we plump for the Denby Greenwich crockery with its green glass goblets and jewel green glaze. A stroke of luck is a cutlery sale. As Laurence's parents want to buy us a canteen, we find a striking modern style and ask for it to be put to one side for us. We really do feel like two kids in a sweet shop and although I'm constantly on the look out for gifts at £10 or less, we build up a list of items that will look lovely in our home. As we sign the paperwork at the end of our session I feel it's been a dream day. It's not just the lovely items we've chosen but that we've done this together.

Finally, as Laurence's mum is keen to choose her outfit I enquire about Debenham's Personal Shopper and book her in for next Monday. I also book an Estee Lauder bridal make-up session for myself. Finally, I apply for a goldcard, promising myself not to use it – well, not too much.

THURSDAY 5TH JUNE

This morning I've had confirmation that Air Jamaica can book us on the Wednesday flight and will issue our tickets. Next, I'm at Browns compiling our list by holding an electronic scanner to each item's barcode. At 11am I rush downstairs for my Estee Lauder appointment and it's the best yet. The girl is far nicer and more natural than most of her ilk and I actually look human at the end of the session. She usefully lists the make-up she has used and I choose my wedding foundation and blusher. This earns me a bonus bag of goodies that will be excellent for our honeymoon: a mini perfume, lipstick, foundation, eye palette, day cream and mascara. Today feels like 10 Christmases one after another.

Back in the wedding department I finish scanning and the assistant successfully downloads the list onto her PC. It feels astonishing to see our gift list laid out on the touch-sensitive PC screen with our names and marriage date at the top. I key in my surname and succeed in bringing up the list and printing it off to show Laurence.

Friday 6th June

It's time to start on the confetti which I want to make myself from rose petals from our garden, so I start gathering my harvest of flowers. I'm using the high speed method of sticking rose petals between two sheets of kitchen towel. I just microwave on High for one to two minutes and they emerge beautifully dry and papery.

Sunday 8th June

At church today we are both startled when Jonathan reads the Banns and suddenly announces our names. This formality makes the wedding even more of a reality than ever. Now I need to get our Banns read in our own parish of Dodleston. Jonathan has

warned us that he absolutely can't marry us without a certificate from our own vicar.

MONDAY 9TH JUNE

Today we both get up at the crack of dawn to rush over and pick up Laurence's parents for the Personal Shopper appointment. Laurence's mum is rather nervous about the whole experience and also self-conscious about being in a wheelchair. The session begins with a question and answer session about my future mum-in-law's favourite colours and her tastes in clothes. While Laurence and his dad go off shopping, we ladies can laze in the cool lounge while the personal shopper collects armfuls of outfits from the shop floor. At last I can tell Laurence's mum that my own mum has chosen a navy blue suit for the wedding, thanks to Lorraine. It may be plain and rather puritanical but it certainly leaves most of the colour palette free for my future mum-in-law. After trying on a range of styles and colours, Laurence's mum chooses a dusky pink suit with a lovely white summer sweater. At this point her sister Edna arrives and together everyone agrees that this is the outfit for her. It is also a thrill to see Laurence return with the big cutlery canteen wrapped and ready and to know that it's our first gift from the wedding list. Later, his parents send us a wedding card with a cheque for £200 'as the cutlery was cheaper than they had anticipated'. His parents are so lovely that I burst into tears.

TUESDAY 10TH JUNE

I contact our local vicar, Jacqui, and she helpfully tells me that she can organise the initial details for the Banns over the phone. She will read them over the next three weeks and then we can get together when she has the certificate ready.

In the evening I have a glorious time putting together an ideas scrapbook. I've got all my bridal magazines out and I'm snipping pictures of bouquets, table settings and hairstyles. I keep thinking of Lorraine's idea of a Victorian theme with wild flowers, roses and hand written cards and at last a clearer picture is emerging.

TIP: *Get into the habit of snipping appealing pictures from magazines to form a 'picture board' of ideas. Add photos and swatches of your outfits, and anything else that helps to build a montage of your wedding.*

MONDAY 16TH JUNE

Lorraine is coming over to view the hall and help order the flowers today. Lying awake at dawn I try to figure out what exactly is bothering me. Well, Lorraine and I have been plotting away for weeks now on our Victorian country theme. And Lorraine, being an absolutely top designer wants to do the best job possible, with the best materials and of course that's going to take …money. I wonder just how much longer I can keep the rising costs of all this from Laurence.

The weather is just glorious again, with a radiant blue sky shimmering above the cornfields. Lorraine arrives, all copper tanned and designer shaded and Laurence and I pile into her BMW to whizz down to the hall. From the outside, it looks amazing. The cottages in Eccleston now have gardens overflowing with old English roses and spikes of frilly hollyhocks. Then we go inside.

Plastic playgroup equipment is scattered across the floor and for the first time I notice that the floor is indelibly marked out for netball or football or whatever. The bare walls are scarred and gouged. Even in this glorious sunshine the room looks utilitarian. Suddenly we all seem to be shivering.

"Oh dear," says Lorraine, surveying the vast magnolia painted walls. "It's so big. I don't remember the walls being so big."

Big? It looks like the Millennium Dome on closing down day. I have to stifle the urge to apologise and grovel. This is going to take a miracle.

"What about that great muslin idea?" I ask.

"I just don't think it'll work. It's too big."

There is a very long silence.

"This place needs painting," Lorraine announces, stating the obvious. "What about hiring it the week before and giving it a lick of paint?"

Now I know what 'a lick of paint' is in the design trade. Michelangelo gave the Sistine Chapel a fancy lick of paint. It took four long years and a lot of sweat and scaffolding.

"I'm not entirely sure that's feasible," I say.

"The paint would cost a lot," chips in Laurence.

"I'll just have to think about it," she says, strolling off with a preoccupied look on her face. Lorraine, like me, is a worrier. A thinker and planner, she needs time and quiet to build her fabulous schemes. And then, what visions emerge – fantastical, stylish, tasteful and bold. I am so proud of her and think often of our playing as girls in a house so poor in furnishings but enriched by our imaginations. Fairy stories, costumes, foreign lands, and myths have all fed the well of her inspiration.

I keep myself busy rummaging in the kitchen and attic. On the lawn I plan four large square tables surrounded by the hall's retro wooden chairs and our own huge Racing Green sun umbrella. I go back inside in trepidation.

Laurence is happy, at least. Having appropriated the large wooden panels for the photography and art exhibition he's planned, he's humming away to himself, completely self-absorbed. The Exhibition, as it becomes known and loved, serves a number of spectacular purposes. It recalls both of our families and their histories, celebrates Laurence's wonderful new artwork, and allows him to inhabit an eerily calm vacuum at the centre of the wedding maelstrom that's spinning uncontrollably around him. Perfect.

Lorraine, meanwhile, is pacing about staring at the yellowing, yawning chasm that the hall has suddenly come to resemble.

"I could try wallpaper." What on earth? We'd have to buy up B & Q.

"Ah, wallpaper," I reply knowingly. Then add, "How's that work?"

"I got the idea from the children's artwork." Around us are some large paper hangings on bamboo. "I could get some gorgeous wallpaper and make paper panels in sections. That would cover the worst of it. Distraction's the thing. I need to draw the eye."

"That sounds wonderful!" I'm not sure what she means but it sounds like the kind of magic words I'm looking for. And if Lorraine thinks it will work, it will work to perfection.

Over a quick lunch in the garden I show Lorraine my scrapbook. I can't believe how useful this is proving, not only to clarify my own ideas but also to show other people the kinds of flowers and table decorations I would like. Then, barely before we've had time to scoff some salad, we're off through the heat haze of lanes to my florist at Hawarden.

PLEASURES TO TREASURE

FRESH FLOWERS

Flowers are a budget item you may not expect to spend much on, but that will organically grow with a life force of their own. To keep the budget down:

- Enlist a keen friend or family member to arrange flowers for you.
- Keep it all extremely simple. Carry lilies or a single rose.
- Borrow from an American tradition: ask close family and friends to each bring a single bloom to your ceremony. Collect the flowers into a ready made bouquet.
- Double up all your flowers by asking the florist to move your pew ends and pedestals to the reception.
- Tell your florist your maximum budget and steer the choices towards cheaper flowers in season.
- Ignore expensive cut flowers in favour of small pots of sweet peas, herbs or silk flowers. Hanging baskets and troughs can look sensational – and you keep them to decorate your home afterwards.
- Hire or borrow bay trees, baskets, pots and topiary. Try your local parks department or garden centre or enlist keen local gardeners.

BUTTONHOLES – *usually only provided for the male members of the bridal party: Carnations: about £3 each*
Roses: about £5 each
Exotic flowers: up to £15 each

CORSAGES – *usually only provided for the female members of the bridal party:*
Spray of rose and freesia: about £10 each
Fresh flower wrist corsage: about £10 each

BOUQUET
Supermarket bouquet of lilies and foliage: from £12
Hand tied bouquet from high street florist: from £25
Deep red roses trimmed with maribou feathers, designer florist: from £70

HEAD-DRESSES
Bridal circlet: from £25
Fake hair flowers, vary by size and quality: £3 – 50

BRIDESMAIDS' FLOWERS
Hand-tied posies from high street florist: from £20
Bamboo baskets filled with lily and fuchsia petals to scatter, designer florist: from £40

RECEPTION
Glass vases with garden grown frothy gypsophilia, high street glass vases: around £10 each
Trailing table arrangement of berried ivy, roses, anemones and lilies, designer florist: from £70

TIP: *Tempting as it is, don't try to arrange your own flowers unless you have previous experience and reliable helpers, or you're going for a rustic look.*

Getting out my list and scrapbook, we get down to business. My bouquet is easy enough as I've got a magazine photo that

Lorraine and Sue approve of and it can simply be copied. The idea is to have a bunch of pink and cream roses hand tied with lace.

"Oh, and I'd like those sort of berry things," I try. "You know, they look like shiny green beads?" Fortunately, there's a photo and they work it out. But pretty soon I find my attempts to keep up with, never mind lead, the conversation are thwarted. I just don't speak the language of flowers. When Lorraine and I were very little girls she had whole books of flowers and could recite every name by heart. I had thought I could tell a delphinium from a daisy but it seems that, like everything else, times have changed even in the innocent world of flowers. Pretty soon, the conversation is going like this:

"I can get Pyrohedronatochanthus."

"What, even in August?" Lorraine is thrilled. "Yes, a few fronds. And some Doxyfloxyate. Just at the edges."

"Then Linoleum for the pew ends. Pink Linoleum."

I staple my lips together and let them get on with it. I always thought that was something you put on hospital floors.

"And bear grass of course."

Lorraine nearly falls of her chair. "No, no! It's a Victorian theme. Too modern. Too spiky. Don't you think, Laura?"

"No spikes," I agree. "Definitely not."

"Think ivy, fern, think soft pink, think Victorian watercolours."

At last there's a question only I can answer.

"And what shape are the pew ends?" Sue asks. I think very hard, recollecting all the Sunday services I've spent staring at the pew in front of me.

"Er, I don't know." Fortunately, she can use a multi-purpose plastic claw shaped thing with a dome of sponge in the middle. Amazing.

The list grows from bouquets to buttonholes, pew ends and pedestals. The number of flowers being flown in from around the world is starting to feel scarily expensive. They each confide to me how impressed they are with each other. What a relief it all is, like being a successful matchmaker. I realise how disappointing it would have been for either of them just to have me to talk to, stuttering and miming away in pidgin flower language.

Finally, we talk about Sue coming over on the day to transfer the pew ends onto the reception tables.

"They're going to look very flat," she confesses.

Miraculously Sue produces her own tall glass vases upon which the pew ends can be attached with net and cleverly concealed putty. It sounds weird, but should look fabulous. The only item she has to research are the bay trees I've set my heart on, after seeing a pair outside Eccleston Church one Sunday morning. They looked so smart with big ribbons tied around them. These will need hiring, but as for the rest – Sue will let me have the costs as soon as she can. I'm thrilled and a bit scared. What we've just ordered sounds dreamily beautiful but what will Laurence say about the cost of it all?

TUESDAY 17TH JUNE

Leonie calls on the phone, interrupting work and sounding as anxious as I feel.

"I can't wait any longer. We need to get this linen ordered – now!"

A clutch at my heart makes me wonder what would happen if we didn't.

Bare trestle tables? Paper napkins? Old copies of the News of the World?

I start to jabber, then remember I've got a list somewhere. It seems to take hours to run through all the variations of cloth needed to cover the round tables, the buffet tables, the gift table and cake table. At my last estimate we have about 63 guests so I plump for 70 places laid with matching cream napkins. Then there are the green cloths for the lawn and the cutlery and glasses to sort out.

THE WEDDING FEAST

CATERING WITH STYLE

- For a sophisticated look, the right linen will set the scene, from heavy linen to metres of informal gingham or cotton prints.
- Sari cloth, velvets and voiles can look beautiful but remember there will be vast quantities of cloth to buy.
- Unattractive chairs can be covered in fabric slips *(covers with choice of coloured sash) from £2.99 per chair.*
- Cost of glass hire varies greatly, from free with your booze (*Supermarket, small deposit plus charges for breakage and washing),* to 10p per wine glass from a caterer to 50p for a fine crystal goblet.
- Tables look lovely if swagged with fabric (*Voile about £10 per metre)* or foliage *(Florist's garland from £40).*
- When choosing cutlery, glassware and linen remember that the heavier the weight, the greater impression of luxury.

Next, as I chat to Leonie, I see I've written 'cake decoration' on my list. In a rare lucid moment it dawned on me that rushing around Sainsbury's for 25 punnets of fresh raspberries on my wedding morning is not a good idea – those red summer fruits don't half leave a stain on cream satin. I've just got to delegate this one.

"You know the summer fruits for dessert?" I ask Leonie.

"Ye-es?"

"Well, I was wondering if you could keep back some fruit, the best fruit really, and just, you know, put it on the cake."

"You mean decorate it?"

"Just put the fruit on it."

"But I won't know what you want."

"I'll send you a photo. It's easy." (Face screwed up at blatant lie. Just looking at pictures of final wedding cake titification brings me out in an icy sweat). "Just have a look. I'll email it over."

"I don't use email." How have I chosen a major supplier who doesn't use email?

"I'll post it," I say firmly, "along with all these measurements. Oh, and there's a little girl with a nut allergy," I add quickly to change the subject.

Phew, I think, as I put the phone down. I clip out a photo of the £400 cake from Slattery's and post it, not a little guiltily, to my unsuspecting caterer.

Laurence gets home in a stinking mood. After some discussions about what Keith should wear, Laurence offered to hire him a best man's outfit in the same style as the formal morning suit he's just decided to wear. (So all those threats to wear a clown suit were a joke, huh?) The men's first foray into the Wedding World has not been a happy one – for Laurence's nerves or the budget.

They have chosen Pronuptia as it is around the corner from Keith and Yvonne's house and they stock masses of traditional plain navy morning coats and pinstriped trousers.

Keith has been in his element trying on all the gear while Laurence looked on in mortification. "He came out of the dressing room in his *underpants*," Laurence tells me in horror. "And there were ladies in the next room!"

I can't help but laugh at this image of Keith stomping about half-dressed.

"And his outfit alone came to £105. So the budget's going to have to pay for all that."

We haven't even got the prices for the flowers yet. And we need three suits hired – for Laurence, Keith and Chris. Now it's my turn to lift my hand to my mouth in horror. Our budget. I can't even bring myself to do the sums.

WEDNESDAY 18TH JUNE

I've been playing around with ideas for a hen night, or rather, what sounds far more domestic and clucky, a hen day. I've had another lucky letter from Cheshire Life to say that I've won a prize for a chef to come round to the house to cook a meal and I've decided it will be the perfect centrepiece of the day.

Next I get the final bundle of gift lists posted after printing them off direct from the Debenhams website. As we both feel terribly apologetic about asking for gifts I send the following letter along with the list:

Following many requests for ideas for Wedding gifts we have decided to draw up a wedding list available from any branch of Debenhams (including Browns of Chester). This includes such items as a set of Denby tableware and various household items, towards which any small contribution would be very much appreciated.

The reference number to give in all cases is ***898343*** *or, if you forget, simply give our surnames, Bloom & Collins. Giving the reference number, whichever way you purchase, means that there is less likelihood of duplication and we don't get five sugar pots and no mugs!*

However, we do not want anyone to feel pressurised into buying a gift. If nothing on the list appeals, a Debenhams gift token would be most appreciated. Alternatively, a more personal item of your own choosing is always welcome.

Laurence and Laura

Nevertheless, we have agreed not to send this to certain guests who are already contributing lots of time and energy to the wedding.

Whilst on the PC I also get my London based sister, Marijke, on board with her delegated task of wine tasting. I send her a potential order list for her to taste at Berry Bros: a couple of cases of sparkling white for Buck's Fizz, Brut Rosé champagne for the toast and three cases of fruity red and four of dry white for general drinking. I tell her I'm sure that should be enough as by my calculations that's about 10 glasses for each person.

THURSDAY 19TH JUNE

I must say I finally do feel a bit fitter and more toned. I love the Clarke diet's super-rich food and am pigging out on extraordinary meals: venison sausages, stilton on toast, jelly and cream, salmon and hollandaise… And I get my reward at the gym – I'm only 3lbs over target. That means I've lost 11lbs since Christmas.

I must have been radiating post weigh-in cheer as I stalked Chester for wedding favours. Spotting an elderly chap blowing streams of bubbles into the air by the Eastgate Clock I buy a couple of bubble guns and tell him I need them for a wedding. So then the chappie throws in a free refill and wishes me luck. It's funny how the world seems so cheery when your mood swings up. I really must be giving off some kind of aura today in the manner of joy filled, slimmed down, imminent bride.

The euphoria had to end, of course, when I called in at the cake supplies shop to hire more paraphernalia. Cake tins for baking are cheap to borrow, but a silver cake stand, though only £7.50 a day to hire, needs a £25 deposit. I ask the shop owner about the sign in her window announcing that their wedding cake business is for sale. It seems that her husband has had enough of wedding cakes.

"It's this fashion for chocolate cakes. No one realises how many hours are involved. He was up all night with one trying to get the chocolate smooth. When he turned up the lady wanted it displayed in front of a sunlit window. He told her it would melt but she wouldn't listen. Like a fire in a wax museum."

Oh dear. Should I be listening to this?

I flick through her catalogues and show her the cake I want to make with white chocolate curls.

"Have you ever made one of those?"

"Ooh, no. Never even tried. White chocolate is very temperamental, you know. Difficult." Hmm, they are professional cake bakers and even they view white chocolate as some kind of unstable nuclear element likely to go off in your face.

This evening I sit down with all my ideas for favours and price them up. Counting up our female guests, I decide to buy 35 favours. Despite the recent trend for men's favours, I've decided to be traditional on this one (in other words, save money).

YOUR DAY, YOUR WAY

WEDDING FAVOURS

The old tradition of giving each guest a piece of 'wedding luck' (historically in the form of a lover's knot ribbon or piece of cake decoration) has burgeoned into providing a small gift to each female (and now even male) guest. Remember that it's not a compulsory item. If you do buy them, price each favour and multiply according to your recipients:

- Make your own favours: a tiny posy of flowers or herbs, home made chocolates or biscuits iced with your names.
- Sweet things are generally popular:
  Two-chocolate ballotin: around £2 each
  Traditional net wrapped Bombonier: from £1.20 each
- More unusual items can echo your theme:
  A country wedding – *Scented drawer sachets: about £3 each*
  Welsh wedding – *Celtic love spoons with ribbons and cards: £1-2 each.*
  Spring wedding – *Mini seed pots: make your own or about £3 each*

Tudor Wedding – *Elizabethan comfits: around £2 each tin*
Historical wedding – *Wrapped soaps: £1-2 each*

I order 42 gold voile drawstring bags from Confetti Online, to fill with the traditional five chocolate dragees in gold foil, which works out at £1.08 per person. At the same time I order a few more table decorations: 24 heart shaped gel candles (vanilla), bulk bag of gold foil chocolate hearts to scatter, scarlet rose petals for the cake and seven boxes of Wedding Trivial Pursuit to put out on the tables as an ice-breaker. I can't believe it when the total bill comes to £102.

SUNDAY 22ND JUNE

My spendthrift ways are happily rewarded when my dad rings. Do I *really* want something from the gift list, he asks, and I feel myself drooping, all crestfallen. Well, he could just buy me a little present, I think, sorrowfully. Or do I want cash instead? I perk up. "Er, the money would be really useful," I say, knowing it's not polite, but yes, to be honest, we could do with it. So he tells me he's putting a cheque for £500 in the post. Feel like crying again. Aren't people good?

I've become addicted to checking out the Tryall Club website to get an instant high from the pictures of swish villas, white beach and romantic pier. What has been worrying is the section on costs – it's £280 half board per person per week. As it's a large security fenced plantation about 12km outside Montego Bay, I realise we can't exactly nip out for dinner. I decide to tell Dad that we'll put the £500 towards booking in half board so we won't be too terrified of bankrupting ourselves in the restaurant. We've also decided to allocate the £200 from Laurence's parents to the village hall hire. I think they like the idea that they have provided the venue for such a big family bash.

Thursday 26th June

Forget the feeling so fit and fantastic mood. At Pilates I've been doing a lot of legwork, *passe developé* as our instructor calls it. It's the exercise you see ballet dancers doing, lifting their legs effortlessly up into the air: flex, point, flex, point. Only ballet dancers don't have big heavy tree trunks on the end of their hips or have hours of wedding shopping trudging to endure afterwards. But I do order my shoes at last. I've plumped for the Rainbow shoes in the Bliss (comfy) range. The ivory satin should be fine and as the heels are a mere 2 inches high I should be able to dance the night away without doing any spectacular tumbling routines. Unfortunately, they have to be ordered and cost £50. Rather expensive for a one-off outing I think, but essential to keep my feet both blister free and in direct contact with the ground as I gallop around the dance floor.

Friday 27th June

The start of a real panic over the budget tonight. I've just ordered the chocolate for the cake, which alone is £38 for 5 kg of Belgian white couverture. Knowing that I've been rather free with the plastic recently (shoes, favours, flowers, the men's outfits) I do a quick tally. Laurence is sitting on the sofa at the other side of the room and I feel myself turning scarlet and hoping he won't ask me why. We have hit £4,000 already and there is so much more still to buy.

I realise I've been heading for this moment right from the start. Our budget is too small – well, it's too small for my idea of a wedding. I want flowers, I want smart suits and lovely food and crisp linen. Call me a spendthrift, but there is only a certain amount of penny pinching I can stand.

So that's how I've arrived at my solution. Our 'official' budget hovers at around £4,000. But the things I really want on top of that I'll have as well. I glance up at Laurence innocently chuckling at a rerun of *The Good Life*. I suppose he's a bit like the Richard Briers character, idealistically trying to be self-sufficient and imposing his daft eco-standards on poor Felicity Kendall. Well, what if Felicity had her own savings, the money she saved from growing all they need in their own back garden? You see, since Laurence paid off half our mortgage, I've noticed a certain amount of extra money sloshing around. Let's call it my Slosh Account. And it is my money, for me to spend as I like. So, whether it's on flowers that will be dead by midnight or the best chocolate in the world that will disappear down people's gullets, I will spend it. It's about pleasure, about dignity and doing it just once in your lifetime. Guiltily, I push my new budget sheet down to the back of my folder – out of sight, out of mind.

SATURDAY 28TH JUNE

My budget calculations have made it even more unavoidable that I make the cake. And after all, I can't forget Laurence's proud announcement that I am going to save £300 by baking my own wedding cake. (Oh, sorry day). Surely with all the gear I'm collecting, I can manage an edible cake?

Tonight, with friends we have my latest prototype cake for

dessert after its test freeze and test defrost. Although I say it myself, the cake is moist, fudgy and rich. Laurence turns to me in front of everyone and says "This is it! Don't change anything. This is the one."

SUNDAY 29TH JUNE

After a heat groggy nap in the afternoon we're lounging about upstairs. Laurence is choosing poems for the wedding, which should be a dreamy way to pass the time, but isn't. I've tried offering him the prepackaged booklets I've kept from bridal magazines and I've even borrowed poetry anthologies and left them on his bedside cabinet. Ever his own person, Laurence leafs through his own books of poetry to review his favourites. He reads a few to me and nothing really clicks for either of us. Then he reads something he loves by Sir Philip Sydney. The gist of the poem is basically 'Don't bother with all that love stuff, it all rots away, and is hardly worth the trouble anyway.'

"But that's about the transience of love," I protest. "And this is my wedding."

"It's not just *your* wedding. I've got a right to choose too!" he storms.

Ooops. I shut up, go downstairs and leave him to it. His wedding too? Now that is a novel concept.

MONDAY 30TH JUNE

Meeting Laurence at the gym I realise that my censoring of wedding issues is continuing apace. It's not that I am actually keeping anything secret from him (well, except my own spending) just

that I tend towards the drip feed method. So today it's time to drip feed the beer. Instead of buying dozens of cans or bottles of beer, Weetwood Brewery will supply a cask, set it up on Friday and dismantle it on Monday, all for around £80. As Leonie said, men love it, especially as they can pull a pint for themselves. Laurence agrees to my ordering this, although he'd like to try the range of beers first. Great.

What I'm keeping bottled up is the wedding insurance. Maybe it's a premonition of a bumpy ride ahead, but my anxiety over our having to cancel is growing. Or is it wishful thinking, given the sensation of a juggernaut speeding towards us at full pelt? If we *had* to cancel because of illness or an accident (the village hall burning down, or my breaking a limb, or irreconcilable differences over poetry) where would that leave us?

GETTING ORGANISED

WEDDING INSURANCE

- Nothing is going to compensate you for having to cancel, but losing all your deposits will rub painful salt in any wounds.
- Wedding insurance generally includes cover for loss, damage or accidents, non-appearance of suppliers and the retaking of all wedding photographs if they don't turn out.
- Some policies offer insurance of wedding presents against accident for up to three months over the whole wedding period – useful if you are transporting porcelain and glass to and from the reception.
- Given factors like alcohol consumption, personal liability insurance is essential. Most policies will pay around £2 mil-

lion to cover any liability arising from accidental injuries, loss or damage to third parties at the wedding.

- Prices of premiums rise roughly in accordance with the amount of money covered:
  Expect to pay around £65 for £7,500 cancellation cover and incrementally more for a costlier wedding
  Marquee cover is often an extra – expect to pay about £5 per £1,000 insured

I go for the Debenhams basic Gold insurance at £60 as it's discounted to goldcard members and offers three months' insurance of all items on the gift list.

Finally, I do my massive To Do list for July. My son Chris arrives back from his New Zealand travels on the 9th August, so I have barely six weeks left to finish everything. I'm so much looking forward to seeing him that I don't want to be some crazed Bridezilla in those final few weeks. So, lots to do over the next few weeks:

MUST DO*:*

Laurence to prepare menus, Orders of Service and all other paperwork (must not nag). Write thank yous as gifts arrive in manner of fantastically formally polite new wife. Find miracle underwear. (Hear basques and suspenders show too many ridges and bobbles through fabric. My researches have uncovered all-in-one white stocking-tights – tights that look like stockings, with 'vents' to show a little thigh flesh – as the perfect smooth, though sadly asexual underwear.)

Decorate garden trug with flowers, ribbons, etc – though not too soon or will die and wilt in style of funerary object. Decide first dance. Actually unsure – can we already dance? Do we need dancing lessons? Is this my

lemming like reaction to American style wedding industry or something I really want? Buy present for Keith (something suitable eg pewter object or something he'd really like eg power tools?) Finalise florist's order (need to add tons more flowers for guests whom I realise might otherwise be offended, and bouquets for people we especially need to thank). Decide table plans, possibly naming tables rather than numbering, eg our favourite holidays:Rome, Naples, Venice, or even places of importance in our lives: Sheffield, Bolton,Ramsbottom. Maybe not…

Get hold of Banns certificate and deliver it to Jonathan – we can't get married without it.

Get rings. Almost forgot those. Can't get married without them.

Do NOT alienate the groom.Definitely can't get married without him.

NO THANK YOUS

TUESDAY 1ST JULY

Unbelievably, it is now only two months until the wedding. Aaaargh! Every time the subject comes up I keep doing that strangled scream and Laurence replies with "Strange girl," and shakes his head sadly. Another good omen is that we both slept through until 7am. I wake from a dream in which I'm unpacking boxes of table decorations for the reception and my gold tea light holders are inside the box where they should be. Not only that, but they looked quite good, actually. So, after all my panicky nightmares about lost dresses and clocks whizzing round like aircraft propellers, maybe I'm not quite as anxious as I think.

Despite the obsessive urge to start my massive To Do list we have time for a chat about the CDs we want to play before Laurence goes to work. He enthusiastically dictates while I scribble lists of our favourite artistes in the manner of a super-keen 1950s stenographer. Soon he gets sidetracked into playing CDs. He puts on some Cuban music (fine) and then some very avant-garde Steve Reich. The opening is lovely and tinkly but then it starts to drone like a jet and I can imagine all The Relatives looking baffled and saying it sounds like aliens landing outside. We also agree to have a folkier CD through the band's amps in the interval of the Ceilidh to keep the atmosphere upbeat.

I've still got to find that obscure Welsh Harpist CD we heard one night on the radio and forgot to write down. I'm also keen to find some Indonesian Gamalan music to reflect my family's heritage from Java.

PARTY TIME

MUSIC

- Check your venue's entertainment licence and test any music systems well in advance of the day.
- Include the favourite music you fell in love to, or that reflects your heritage or interests.
- Avoid performers or DJs who tell you they know best. It's your wedding, not theirs.
- Alternatively, ask your guests for favourite tunes and compile a playlist so everyone hears at least something they like.

Your own music system and supply of music: Nil

A local DJ supplied with a playlist: £100-250

Live band: £100+ for local musicians, up to £1,000+ for a top band

A full sounds and lights show to a professional club level: £500+

A celebrity DJ like Fatboy Slim: £10,000 per hour

TIP: *Delegate overseeing any amplified music to a 'sober' and responsible person equipped with spare fuses, batteries or even a whole spare system.*

I also manage a bit of rapid-fire decision making. We've agreed on two hymns: 'Jerusalem' and 'Be Thou My Vision'. Then on Sunday in church Laurence turned to me and said "Let's have this one as well," in the middle of some vaguely pleasant song with a lot of allelujahs. I looked it up in the hymn book we've borrowed from church and it's very long and I doubt anyone will ever have sung it before. I suggest a few alternatives and of course Laurence says, "How does that go?" So as he sits back smirking on the sofa I have to tunelessly warble the openings of 'The King of Love My Shepherd Is,' and 'Praise My Soul The King of Heaven'. There was a time when he used to believe my rock chick credentials as a member of an all girl band just might have included singing on stage. Not now. Singing in tune is not one of my talents and my last shred of street cred – and dignity – have disappeared in the same direction as my pose as a modern post-feminist intellectual who scoffs at all that girly bridal stuff.

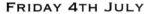

FRIDAY 4TH JULY

Today I have a horrible crisis. It starts at my gym class. I'm happily chatting to a fellow Pilates classmate about not losing enough weight when she says, "Have you thought about eating less?" Only she delivers it with a bit of a sarcastic twang to my ultra-paranoid ears. Yeah, yeah, I say. I'm on this Dr Clarke, you know, low-carb thing. Only then, I think, that's it. Eat less. Then I weigh myself and to my horror I've put on 3lbs.

Anxieties crawl forth and multiply from the black pit of my unconscious. I have to change my top three times before I can leave the gym changing rooms and keep imagining myself plodding up to the bridal shop to pick up my shoes looking like Mrs Blobby. What am I doing wrong? Eat less, exercise more. It's that simple. Only somehow it isn't that simple.

The lowest point of my mood strikes in Marks and Sparks, inside the changing cubicle. I put on a swimsuit that is the right blue colour and the right shape, only instead of looking like a Caribbean Queen I look like someone's Gran circa the 1950s. Horrible. Of course, once you're in a vicious downwards spiral, things get worse and worse. I can just see a bit of ashy blonde hair that could be … *grey!*

Things do get a bit better. I buy a nice lacy bra (cream rather than flesh coloured) and a big pair of unsexy 'pull your tum in' tights. I'll just stick the garter on those and all the fancy frilly stuff can be packed away for the honeymoon.

SUNDAY 6TH JULY

After church Jonathan suggests we have a word with John, the organist. My choice for walking down the aisle, Vivaldi's 'Primavera', is thankfully in his book but we are less certain about the rest of the music. Eventually, by pointing out music we think we recognise and John playing a few bars, we make our choices. As well as confirming that our original two hymns are plenty, John suggests we choose a piece or two for the choir to sing while we're signing the register. I scribble all this down anxiously, knowing I need to draft the Order of Service next. I also realise that I haven't actually budgeted for the extra £227 for bell-ringing, the organists, verger and choir. Oops!

The Wedding Service

Music

- Check any unusual choices with your minister. Many will be very liberal but, on the other hand, will not want to undermine the solemnity of the service.
- For a secular wedding service you won't be allowed any hymns or songs which make reference to God. Again, check if you're unsure.
- Traditional wedding music can be sampled via downloads off the internet, on loan from libraries or even as free CDs with classical music or bridal magazines.
- Well chosen soloists, choirs or even your kid brother on guitar, all make the service more personal and meaningful for those present:

  Soprano soloist: about £200 for a couple of numbers
  Church choir: about £100
  Church organist: about £30
  Bell-ringers: about £60

Wednesday 9th July

Laurence has been very busy with work lately. Well, that's what I'm putting his irritation down to. But there's more to it and our friction is really centred on the hen party. I've asked him to let me and the girls have Sunday alone here and he's not happy about it. After all, Sunday is his big rest day and being banished to Sheffield is not the same as recharging here. I do feel for him, but what can I do? Typically, we don't row and clear the air but avoid each other in resentful silence. I will not give in. I draw the line at having the groom at my hen party.

Thursday 10th July

We both feel just awful this morning, after sleeping badly in the incredible heat and my poor Laurence suffering from hay fever. Thankfully, we make up at 5am and so have at least recovered that serene equilibrium when we love each other so much that nothing else really matters.

Later, I pick up my shoes from the Bridal House. They are quite plain but pretty, with cross-over straps and a neat satin heel. After testing them in the changing room I get talked into buying a matching bag.

"It should be £20," the assistant says, apparently pulling a number out of the air and doubling it. Twenty? It's only a bit of taffeta with ribbons attached. "I'll give it to you for £15," she concedes.

It isn't at all like the artful little numbers I've spotted at Accessorise or Monsoon. But as I hold it up at the window, I can see that miraculously, it does match the swatch of my dress. Oh, and I'm writing a cheque for the shoes anyway. The trouble is, all these choices become bewildering in the end. You find yourself in just one too many shops, you feel vulnerable and you just capitulate to the domineering force of some wedding harpy's will. Very strange.

Nevertheless, as I walk back through the hot dusk I can't help but feel a little proud of my huge white shiny Bridal House of Chester bag. Every day the reality is getting closer. I'm getting married. I really am.

Dressed For Success

Bridal Shoes

Maybe it's the Cinderella story but the whole concept of wedding shoes gets many a bride madly excited. Brides spend an average of £86 per pair but it is easy to spend an awful lot more on those once in a lifetime crystal slippers:

Strappy, elegant designer shoes like Jimmy Choos: £350 +
Crystal beaded ivory courts from a wedding specialist: £200+
Plain ivory satin wedding shoes (often dyeable): about £50
High street strappy diamante sandal: from £30

TIP: *Just remember that despite promising yourself you will dye them, most wedding shoes are never worn again.*

Saturday 12th July

My hen weekend has dawned hot, hot, hot. This morning I'm off to the hairdresser's for my first trial with tiara. Unfortunately, Clare has moved location to the village of Farndon, which is some 20 minutes drive away. On balance, I've decided to stick with Clare rather than the hotel as she is experienced, cheery and also a fount of knowledge on all things bridal. Presenting her with a clipping from a magazine, Clare says the style in the picture will be no problem. After washing my hair, she wraps it in velcro rollers, tongs it and pins it up in barrel curls around the tiara. At the back she lets a big mass of curls tumble down which looks rather pretty.

Next, a massive boost of success at the gym. After all that cream and nuts and cheese I've lost 3lbs! At a mere 2lb over target, I feel such a surge of energy I can hardly drag myself off the machines and home.

I get home and of course Laurence is still here.

"You look about 19," he exclaims. What a man.

And then, "You look beautiful." I want to marry this man – now.

I'm not too sure about the style myself, but I do feel very special and massively excited. Sadly, Laurence is still not excited about being banished to Sheffield.

PARTY TIME

HENS AND STAGS

- New twists on traditional lewd 'dos' include:
  themed club nights – *Cabaret Shows: from £20 per person*
  pub crawl party pack with L-plates, veil and lots of 'dares' for the bride – *Hen night kit (badges, L-plates, dares): around £10*
- Girly nights in can veer from the tame (book a beautician) to the cringeworthy (Ann Summers lingerie and sex toys party).
- Weekends on the piste, top spa breaks or hunting and shooting weekends may sound stylish, but if you aren't picking up the tab, resentment from less well-heeled guests is inevitable.
- 'Hag' parties (hens and stags combined) are the latest, less riotous fashion. Cocktails bars, comedy clubs and casinos make great combined party venues.

TIP: *Make it very clear to your more responsible friends exactly what you don't want to happen – such as a male stripper in front of your prudish boss.*

SUNDAY 13TH JULY

I start the morning by preparing a fresh and healthy lunch. After hoovering, cleaning and laying the table outside everyone arrives at around noon – my sisters Marijke and Lorraine and 'usherette' Yvonne. It's a shame there are only four of us but sadly my prize dinner is only for four people and to be honest, this smaller group suits me. The weather is perfectly sweltering and everyone enjoys chatting over lunch. Next, we go off to Erddig, my favourite historic house. Yet it is so hot inside the house that today Erddig's chief glories are the gardens. We wander happily through avenues of tumbling sweet peas, roses and clematis, enjoying the fierce sun and long views over the Welsh hills.

Soon it is time to get back for our chef's arrival at 5.30pm. We manage to cool off under showers and change in a lovely, frantic rush of perfumes and silks. Outside, I give my jewel glass tealight holders an outing, hanging them in the laurel hedge. Meanwhile, Mark Robertson, our chef, is getting busy in the kitchen while his assistant lays the table with fresh linen, and smart cutlery and crockery. Marijke produces our wines, provided gratis by Berry Bros for us to sample along with some tasting notes. We discuss the wine order and I agree to a £143 surplus over our £540 prize limit. Tonight, who cares? Finally, Lorraine produces a bottle of champagne that we drink chilled with our canapés. This really is the life!

The meal Mark produces is simple but beautifully cooked and presented. It is so wonderful to sit outside my own and Laurence's home in the candelight on a balmy evening being served delicious food and wine with three people I am so fond of. The conversation ranges from male strippers (thank God no one booked one), children, reality TV, writing, and of course, weddings.

Naturally, the conversation drifts onto our non-reception and non-speeches. My sisters don't approve.

"There has to be some sort of focal point," Marijke insists.

"But Laurence doesn't want that sort of formality. I don't think I do either."

I'm beginning to feel the dreaded pressure of family expectations weigh upon us.

"That's not what we mean," Lorraine interjects. "It's not about formality. It's about sincerity."

"I know," I admit. "I feel we should say a big thank you to everyone. But not those sick joke speeches. Laurence would rather die."

Everyone agrees that there needs to be a moment at the wedding when we communicate something, though I'm not sure exactly what, about how we feel. I agree. The trouble is, as I say, "It's entirely up to Laurence. It is his wedding too." Despite the girlie scoffing at this, I know I'm right. One thing about the dynamics of my relationship with Laurence is that I cannot tell him what to do. I can suggest, I can even seek to persuade, but I cannot tell. I find myself mulling over the 'sincerity' theme of this conversation more and more. Like grit in a shoe, it just won't go away.

Wednesday 16th July

The weather is still radiantly hot, in fact so hot that it is difficult to think or move or in any way engage my brain on work. By early afternoon I give up on serious work and armed with a sketch pad, I set off for Eccleston church.

As I arrive, it is 2.47pm. So, as I crunch the gravel between the lime trees leading to the church door, the bell tolls out 3 o'clock. It's exactly the time I'll be walking up the avenue in almost six weeks' time. I imagine wearing my dress and the long train trailing behind me. It all feels so strange and marvellous.

Sitting alone in the cool stone and shadows it comes to me that I am trying to steal back some magic that eluded me in my youth. Like so many people, my early life was troubled; by too much hard work and disappointment, the ekeing out of money and squandering of time and health. And now, by sheer effort of will, I'm going to make it happen. My beautiful lost day. My triumph of hope over disappointment. My wedding day.

Off to Chester and the cake shop to pick up the 6 and 9 inch tins. Whilst being served I notice a huge three tier chrome cake stand high on a shelf. It is not the most attractive stand but I've heard too many stories about wedding cakes collapsing – 'it was so emotional that even the cake sank into tiers'. So I've hired the stand for £15 and bought three thick silver cake boards, so each tier fits firmly on its board and sits on the appropriate tier of the stand. The ugly chrome arms can be disguised with ribbons, ivy or rosebuds.

Tonight I at last tackle baking the actual wedding cake. I had imagined baking my own wedding cake to involve daintily weighing and sifting in sheer Domestic Goddess like bliss. Instead, I feel more like some Below Stairs drudge heaving huge bowls of mixture in and out of the fiery furnace oven.

I'm also horrified by how much I'm spending:-

	£
White couverture chocolate	38
Value plain chocolate	3
Flour, butter, eggs, sugars, etc	12
Cake stand and tins hire	13.50
Dowels and boards	5
Kahlua liqueur	11
Organic cocoa	7
Cream	5
Baking strips/tier cutter	8
Chrome cake stand hire	15
TOTAL	**117.50**

My grumpiness reaches a climax when I pop out for yet more double cream and my shopping bag bursts and drips unseen all over our hall carpets. I am furious about the waste of cream, about having to make a return trip to buy more, and just about making the whole ridiculous cake in general. Meanwhile Laurence is furious about the fat stains all over the carpet. We are both tired and moody. I mop up the kitchen floor. He swears at our ruined carpets. I am sick of it all.

SATURDAY 19TH JULY

In the evening we have our best man, Keith and two ushers (Fran and Yvonne) over. I get the least successful of last week's prototype cakes out of the freezer as dessert and when I serve it with vanilla ice cream it is – okay. I remember the last time I served it and everyone said it was wonderful, fantastic, The Cake. Did I do anything different? No. And this is the cake I've made tons of, all those massive tiers now sitting in the garage freezer. No. I must resist the temptation to bake it all again. That way lies madness…

Back at our dinner party, Yvonne says she has read her photocopied list of usher's duties and can reel them off, down to providing umbrellas. Keith is understandably a little more restrained, though we laugh about some of the traditionally prescribed duties such as getting a hair cut – Keith has a long ponytail down his back. Also, he says he isn't going to 'ensure the groom's car is serviced'! Shame. We have a quick run down on Laurence's whereabouts on the day and everyone insists he stay elsewhere overnight, at a friend's house or his parents'. The trouble is – he definitely wants to stay at home on our wedding eve. Why do people love to tell the bride and groom what to do?

We also confirm lots of tricky bits that need deciding: that we'd like Keith to pick up and return the men's outfits, that Fran will sort out the buttonholes and flowers and Keith and Laurence will drive to the church together in Laurence's car and leave it overnight. Regarding the taxis, we do some preliminary thinking about times. Keith seems to think that as the band finishes at 11pm, everyone needs to be out by 11.30pm so he can lock up. Good idea. I'm thrilled that everyone is pooling their valuable ideas and energies. What a team!

While we're both on a high it seems the right time to mention the budget as we wind down for bed. After all, I *have* made the cake. Laurence goes quiet.

"How much do you need, now?" he finally asks. I shrug and he offers a cheque for £500. If I match that, we've now got £3,500. How can I tell him that's nowhere near enough?

MONDAY 21ST JULY

Chris rings from New Zealand. He'll be here on the 9th August and I'm longing to have all my wedding planning finished by then. This gap year working visa has given him such confidence and he enthuses about New Zealand. We also have a laugh about the wedding when I apologise (as is my habit) and say, "I'm sure you don't want to hear about all that." "But it's all new and exciting to me," he protests. "I *do* want to hear all about it."

Next, Lorraine rings with the brilliant news that she has virtually completed all the silk flower arrangements for the window sills in the hall. She has also tracked down 10 rolls of Victorian style wallpaper in old gold with pink roses. I offer her cash but she refuses – what can I do to thank her for all this? I've asked our photographer to take shots of the empty hall, place settings, and flower arrangements, so she can use them for her business. Also, I've added three bouquets to our florist's order to present to Lorraine and our two mums on the day.

I can't think of any other ways to thank Lorraine, except to visualise myself drawing everyone's attention to the beautifully decorated village hall and to tell them that this has all been transformed by my wonderful sister. Bride's speeches seem to be quite the fashion and after hearing my sisters' little lecture on sincerity, I think I'll have a go. I just hope I don't get too nervous. I may need to hide some little prompt cards in my bag.

SATURDAY 26TH JULY

I cannot believe my spending this week:

	£
2 rolls ribbon for trug and possibly cake	7
Artificial ivy for cake stand	6
40 gold and burgundy thank you cards	16
3 white chocolate mice (possible fun decoration for cake if all else fails!)	2
Tooth whitening kit (can't afford dentist job at £200)	10
Tights	15
Bridesmaids' thank you cards, cakes boxes, gift wrap	11
TOTAL SPEND	**£67**

Then today, I got the florist's quote: £550. This includes the topiary trees and the new order for bouquets, extra buttonholes and bridesmaids' headdresses, but nevertheless, it is a whopping £200 over budget.

SUNDAY 27TH JULY

Today I feel time really hurtling towards our last month. And how do I feel? I'm on that section of the proverbial roller coaster where you know the end is in sight but you still have to face the worst dizzy heights and stomach lurching lows. When I realise that it will all be finished in little over a month, I feel a mixture of relief at getting our old life back and, unbelievably, a kind of regret that all the excitement will be over.

Nevertheless, I won't be sorry to be rid of my stress symptoms. I have been obsessing over the tiniest detail. It seems that once the Big Things are all in place like booking the band and caterer, everything shifts down to the next level of detail. So instead of wondering how to bake the cake, I am now at the Next Level of wondering how to decorate the tops of the cakes. I mean, how trivial is that? Yet at 1.40am this seems the hugest question in the world, an absolutely critical point.

TUESDAY 29TH JULY

I learn today that all the planning in the world can't give you control over your world. I wake up feeling exhausted and red raw with anxiety. I can't believe how much there still is to do and yet each day I've been chipping away.

Crucially, I make an urgent appointment at the Ring Workshop outside Oswestry to choose our wedding rings. Recent forays into Chester, although successful in getting 75% of our men's hire sorted out, have failed totally in our mission to find our rings. I had imagined that it would take about 10 minutes to buy them but after trying dozens of jewellers, Laurence declared that they were all either too boring or flashy or didn't flatter his fingers. So in the end I didn't buy one either, as I would prefer two matching rings. I've tracked down the Ring Workshop as a place that individually designs and casts rings, so fingers crossed they can find something Laurence approves of.

Finally, just as we are relaxing together tonight, the phone rings and Laurence casually picks it up. His mum is in tears as she tries to explain that Kalong, Laurence's sister-in-law, is in hospital after a car accident. After setting off to pick Laurence's dad up from his weekly club outing, the car swerved down a bank into the river. I feel a spasm tighten across my chest as Laurence rings his brother to find out the details. Rodney tells us that only the air bag saved her and she had to escape from the flooded car and haul herself up the bank of the river in the dark. This certainly puts our own trivial anxieties into perspective as we wait for further news.

Wednesday 30th July

Today we set off on our long and tedious journey to Oswestry, miles and miles down country lanes to an odd looking craft centre near the Shropshire Hills. Thankfully, Laurence is immediately impressed by the Ring Workshop's founder, Mark. The whole process seems to take hours involving Laurence trying on hundreds of rings in different shapes, metals and designs.

Pleasures To Treasure

Wedding Rings

- Grooms spend an average of £280 and brides £296 on a wedding ring.
- Any ring and any stone can make a beautiful wedding ring. Make it personal to you by choosing a birthstone, unusual style or having a family gem reset.
- Some women object to being 'marked as unavailable' and opt for no ring or exchange alternative gifts or jewellery.
- His and Hers wedding rings are increasingly popular – and expensive. Current fashions are for matching platinum and white gold bands set with diamonds.
- The most important factors are durability, practicality and that you'll treasure it forever.

9 carat gold court ring: under £100
Platinum court wedding ring: about £250
Diamond solitaire set in platinum: £1,500-3,500 dependent upon the stone

The good news is that Laurence has chosen a stunning white and yellow gold band with a darker yellow groove and I've chosen a simple gold band to fit around my engagement ring. We are having our names and our wedding date engraved inside them both but Mark does warn us that we have left it terribly late. He hopes to have the rings cast and ready by the week before the wedding (last minute horror) and the total cost is £430 (budget horror).

At home we find good news waiting for us as Kalong is recovering well, despite the car being entirely written off. I seem to have developed a kind of surface calm in the face of all this emotional buffeting. Then again, I do have something new and huge to worry about. It's my thank you speech. I've looked at a few model brides' speeches on the internet and they look very long and scary. What if I dry up? Or faint with nerves? Or simply ruin my whole wedding day due to an all consuming dread of public speaking?

THURSDAY 31ST JULY

I have a banging all day headache (no doubt combination of wedding cake chocolate testing, low-carb kipper kedgeree and bride's speech nerves attack). Headache leaps up ten notches to migraine level after checking the budget. Horror of horrors, the official budget is now … £7,400! Well, that does include the long since paid for engagement ring and some items actually paid for by others. Nevertheless, it's actually £4,200, which is £700 more than the £3,500 currently in my savings account. I've secretly decided to bite the bullet and pay as much of the £700 overspill as I can from my slosh account. Despite this, today I buy some tempting jewellery (Jon Richards crystal bracelet (£18.99), crystal ear studs, (£10.99), plus another £9.99 on sparkly hair springs to twinkle in my hair from Claire's Accessories).

Today I'm so jittery about the 'non-speeches' section of the day that I bravely tackle Laurence about it. I tell him I can no longer stand this important part of our wedding day being left until the last minute. If people are going to read, they need to know what they are going to say. The upshot is that he rings Keith.

"Sorry," Laurence reports back. "The answer is no. He doesn't do public speaking."

We can hardly blame Keith as when Laurence asked him to be best man, it was made very clear to him that there would be no speeches. Then, another shock. Liz, Yvonne's mum, may not be able to speak either. Liz is a remarkable lady, an academic and writer who had informally agreed to read a poem as the cake is cut, and then later say a few kind words about us. Since agreeing, she has suffered a health scare and won't have her test results until Saturday. As she is planning to fly over from Canada next Thursday, all her plans are now uncertain. Obviously, our first concern is her health and beside that, our wedding is insignificant.

So I write a first draft of a thank you speech that will just have to be read by *me* if no one else will do it. After all, I've ordered the bouquets and feel someone should stand up to thank the assembled multitude. But before I know it, I've written a whole side of A4 just thanking the main bridal party for their help. I read it out loud to myself and it seems to take a heart pounding eternity to get through. No, no, no! I really do not want to put myself through the agonising build up of standing up and delivering all this. Yet I would love to thank people personally. I feel like my head is in a vice. Get my head outta here!

MUST BUY:

Buy soaps and hand creams for the ladies loos – bound to give expensive country house hotel feel and distract from child size toilets and irksome primary school type coat pegs. Another pair of wedding tights (as bound to burst out of first pair if no spare). Must hunt down fab honeymoon nightwear (seeking happy medium between asexual cotton jim-jams and soft porn wisps of nylon from Ann Summers). Hanging baskets for inside the hall. Evergreen branches to hang on rafters (should be cost free but is one allowed to lop off tree branches in the lane? Maybe could go branch felling at night to avoid farmer and save budget?) Gallons and gallons of orange juice but trickily must be cheap while not tasting cheap. Lucky bags for all the children, though must intensively swot up on children's popular culture post 1992 to avoid faux pas involving Tellytubbies or similar lucky bags given to mortified 12 year olds.

MUST DO:

Start writing thank you cards in manner of imperfect but not utterly hopeless new wife. Prepare a detailed minute by minute time plan of The Day and post to all (so won't need to face people if suffering massive pre-wedding stress attack). Keep up (unbelievably time consuming) beauty regime in optimistic hope can still transform self into lithe, tanned beauty in one (Aaargh!) month. Lose weight! (Try eating less? A novel approach but worth trying.) Make vast amounts of white chocolate curls. (Try eating fewer test curls of chocolate? Novel but almost certainly impossible). Deliver Banns certificate and order of service to Jonathan for approval – or can forget all the rest.

MUST NOT:

Obsess over bride's speech to point of having to be certified. Possibly just need a voice coach, valium, vodka – or could I pre-record it all and mime?

MY WEDDING, MY NIGHTMARE

FRIDAY 1 AUGUST

The final countdown! Rang our vicar Jacqui about the Banns certificate and made an appointment for next Tuesday. Started final To Do lists for August. Chris will be here on the 9th so very little time left.

Tonight we took a long walk in the Welsh hills. The empty lanes were beautiful in the sunshine and as dusk fell the silhouette of the hill fort, Moel Famau, stood high and magical as wild birds circled overhead. After a deliciously high-carb dinner at the pub in Cilcain (prawn curry and sticky toffee pud) we travelled back through high hedged lanes while Laurence told me tales about his childhood and youth amongst these beautiful hills. It feels so good to get away and just be ourselves for a few hours.

TUESDAY 5TH AUGUST

Almost overheating the PC with activity today. First, I started my giant Time Plan (Appendix 1) an hour by hour schedule of the day and the build up to it. I intend to give this out to all the key players and I'll also need it myself to keep track of all the details like furniture deliveries, picking up keys, transport, and so on. The

Order of Service is also ready today, as Laurence has agreed to Shelley's poem 'Love's Philosophy' being read by Fran in church. Finally, I hammer out the Ceremony Box List (things the best man and ushers need to take to the church):

Take to the church

- Wedding rings
- Buttonholes
- Bubble guns and refills
- Confetti
- Seating plans
- Guest book and pen
- 100 orders of service
- Spare copies of photography schedule, Time Plan and poems

Team Management

Getting Others Organised

It is worth listing every item you will need on the day as well as emergency back-up items (*see Wedding Day Emergency Kit, Appendix 2*). Delegate essential items between responsible guests:

- The most commonly forgotten items are: rings, ties, ring pillow, garter, guest book and pens, and bridesmaids' shoes.
- Every supplier present on the day needs a written schedule of events and times.
- A responsible person needs to carry your address book containing all suppliers' contact details.

- Ask someone practical to keep an eye on decorations and bring along sellotape, string and blu-tack.
- Assign someone to deal with left over food and floral decorations.
- Select a responsible usher or family member to take care of any gifts received.

Guest book, hand-decorated: £10-25
Ring pillow: about £10, or if embroidered with couple's names £25+
Printed and corded Orders of Service – per 100: about £100-200
Bubble guns: about £5 each
Bubble machine hire: £15-25 per day

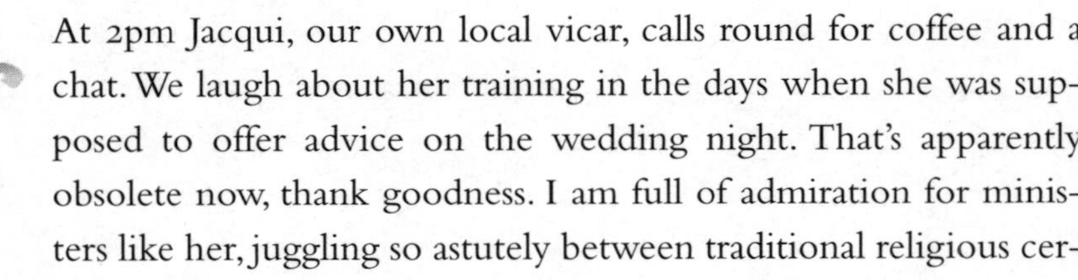

At 2pm Jacqui, our own local vicar, calls round for coffee and a chat. We laugh about her training in the days when she was supposed to offer advice on the wedding night. That's apparently obsolete now, thank goodness. I am full of admiration for ministers like her, juggling so astutely between traditional religious ceremony and the fretful demands of some modern couples.

WEDNESDAY 6TH AUGUST

I've discovered the long term weather forecast on the internet and despite the unending glorious summer a miserable grey cloud icon pops up for 30th August. Please don't let it rain, I pray. The thought of all this hard work and organisation being ruined by rain makes me feel physically sick.

It is hard to imagine rain as we take another day out to hear folk singer Kate Rusby at Gawsworth Hall. It's a wonderful concert, and so nice to be alone and relaxed with Laurence. Yet as we arrive home I have a nasty feeling of coming back to earth and all our worries as we walk in the door. The phone is flashing with a message – but it's only Chris ringing from Auckland to say he's boarding his flight via Bangkok. So sorry to have missed his call but so excited that he's finally flying back home.

Thursday 7th August

My friend Martin from Accrington rings. He is happy to read our chosen John Cooper Clarke poem 'I Wanna Be Yours' (hooray) but there are problems with his getting the bus down to Chester (Oh dear). We've already arranged for him to stay over with Yvonne and Keith on our wedding night. Now, having just checked the bus timetables, he tells us he has nowhere to stay on our wedding eve, either. I feel myself tensing at the thought of having another visitor staying over. I've heard too many stories about bride's houses being full of guests and relatives and selfish bridesmaids and everything collapsing into chaos and tears.

I have to be blunt and say that it just isn't feasible for him to stay here. I also explain that it really is Keith and Yvonne's decision whether he can stay an extra night. It seems incredible that something so small in the scheme of things can make me feel so exasperated. Why have we been left to sort this out just three weeks before the wedding? Every molehill added to my task list feels like a mountain this month.

Friday 8th August

Ups and downs all day. The downs:

We've been concerned about Laurence's elderly parents all

week while they are away on holiday in Eastbourne. There is this terrific heatwave to contend with, it's an unfamiliar place for them and their phone calls have not been reassuring. Last night we heard that Laurence's mum fell on her wrist and it could be broken. It's turned black and a pharmacist has recommended she has it x-rayed.

Then, even worse, Laurence's cousin Anne rings to say that her husband Peter has had a serious stroke. Their circumstances sound truly dreadful and I'm fearful of how she can care for him once he returns from hospital this week.

Looking at our table seating I feel tearful as I wonder who will actually make it to the wedding...

Finally a couple of up moments:

After pondering our Accrington pal's travel problems I get onto the net and quickly find an alternative route for him to travel on our wedding morning. And the wine has arrived from Berry Bros. It looks gorgeous, especially the pink champagne in classy art nouveau bottles.

SUNDAY 10TH AUGUST

Chris is here and he is so funny and relaxing to be with: a breath of pure Kiwi oxygen in our overheated atmosphere. Yesterday we went to Pronuptia and got him kitted out in his morning suit, which looked fabulous.

Dress For Success

Men's Hire

- If the bridal party live in different locations you will need a national supplier such as Moss Bros, Pronuptia or Debenhams to co-ordinate the hire.
- Check out the quality of cloth, choice of styles and cost of any alterations.
- The average spend on the groom's outfit is £197. It is the small accessories that add up:
  Navy morning coat and waistcoat: £80
  Pinstriped trousers: £17
  Wing collar shirt: £8
  Coloured cravat and handkerchief: £6.50
  Shoes: £7
  Cufflinks: £2.50
  Accidental damage insurance: £6
  Morning dress – total hire per person: £126

Having looked at prices, the groom may decide it's almost as economical to buy:
Beige linen suit: £100-200
Wine coloured velvet suit – off the peg: £600
Bespoke suit made for the occasion: £800+

Another bonus is that Chris genuinely wants to know about the wedding. Recently, though, I have noticed that Laurence shuts us down, wearily saying, "that's enough about the wedding, let's talk about something else." The sparks only ignited this afternoon when Laurence and I revised the table seating. We spent 10 minutes rejigging Laurence's family tables; a frustrating task for me as I don't know them all.

THE WEDDING FEAST

FAMILY SEATING

The traditional seating plan is a 'top table' with the couple at the head and mums and dads, bridesmaids and groomsmen, all ranged according to rules of etiquette. Modern twists on wedding seating deal with the realities of step-parents and family splits with more subtlety:

- Place each set of parents (or each parent and new partner) as hosts on different tables.
- Group guests so that everyone knows at least one other person on the table or has an immediate common bond.
- Children may be happier seated apart on their own table if a child minder is employed to care for them.
- However you plan your table seating, an eraser will prove useful. If it gets very tricky, try writing everyone's name on a plastic cup and swizzing them around in different combinations.

TIP: *Don't chicken out of allocating seating if you are providing a sit down meal. From the guests' point of view it is irritating and thoughtless. If you don't want to allocate seats, make it clear that you would like people to mix and switch tables informally so there is no confusion.*

Write-on placecards: £2 for 10

Designer placecards – Feather trimmed and printed; from £2 each

Having done that, I feel I've earned the chance to raise one issue of my own.

"Just one last thing. When Yvonne, Keith and Liz come over tomorrow night I'd like to hand out the detailed Time Plan."

Laurence looks at me as if I've suggested serving vegetarians a meal of disguised pork pie. "Well, be careful how you do it."

"What do you mean?"

"Well, I don't want it to be like a meeting. Don't just hand them out. People don't like being told what to do."

I feel offended. Maybe I don't like being told what to do, either.

"Well, it is a meeting. A team meeting."

"You know, just be sensitive how you do it."

I'm thinking – as if anyone's sensitive to my feelings! I'm just the drudge who does all the work and feels like she's being marked *nul points* all the time.

"Well, okay then I won't hand them out. I know, let's just have a shambles with no one knowing when anything is happening. We can just let it all happen spontaneously on the day. Do a kind of experiment to see how chaotic we can make our wedding day."

He looks furious. "I don't want to talk about this any more."

"Listen, I've spent months organising all of this. I don't want a shambles because no one knows what to do."

"Just stop this. I just want to get away."

My voice cracks. "I just want some support for this. I do all this work and I feel you just don't support me."

I storm out with my heart thumping and great waves of fury pounding through me. The Incredible Hulk has nothing on my rage. Honestly, I could pull a few oak trees out by the roots, I'm so mad. After all, I am *very* premenstrual. It's the most horrible feeling, like toxic fireworks exploding in my veins. I know that Laurence hates confrontation but I just couldn't stop the poison exploding out.

STRESS BUSTING

I'M DRIVING MYSELF CRAZY!

It could be that awkward bridesmaid who won't wear a royal blue ruff or your groom who refuses to wear a smart suit. You're going crazy! Don't they realise it's your wedding day?

- Stop right there and take 10 deep breaths. As I know too well, the pre-wedding build-up feels like you've morphed into a comic book monster with hormone problems. A wedding is stressful enough without saying things you may bitterly regret. Hard as it is to imagine – life and relationships will go on, long after the wedding.
- Instead of turning into a drama queen, consider modelling your behaviour on a calm and gracious bride-to-be – more Grace Kelly, less Bridezilla.
- Listen hard to other people's ideas and why they prefer lilac to royal blue. Simply by acknowledging their point of view you may defuse the situation. Listen out for chances to win/win.

The upshot is that Chris and I went out on our own, but even so it took me ages to calm down. Before I left, Laurence and I made up slightly and kissed goodbye but I knew we both needed time apart.

In the end, I did just hand out the Time Plans and it was okay. I made a joke about being really hyper over The Plan and said I'd welcome their ideas. Liz said it was really useful, Yvonne that it was really organised. Keith asked for a copy for Fran. So what? World War III didn't break out, did it?

Wednesday 13th August

Another day of shocks. As Chris is only here for a month I have rashly agreed to lend him my car so he can take a trip around England (and escape The Wedding Asylum with his sanity intact). So today I did some last shopping and came back laden like, well – like a woman who's getting married in 17 days and won't have a car for the next 10! I can only describe myself as haemorrhaging money on gifts, holiday clothes, jewellery, soft drinks, lingerie and decorations.

Smart Shopping

Sales And Seasons

It's said that the longer your wedding preparations, the more you will spend. I've also been told that the more you spend, the shorter the marriage. However long your lead-up, the final weeks can do serious damage to your wallet:

- Ask yourself, each time you shop, if you could hire or borrow a similar item.
- Seriously consider doing without the 'Going Away' outfit that currently averages at £133.
- A piece of family jewellery, borrowed headdress or antique veil could save much of the £297 spent on these items by the average bride.
- Agree to forego the expense of giving gifts to each other.

Got home and saw Chris off to his grandma's, knowing he will have a lovely time being indulged. Laurence has been bothered by incessant phone calls from work about the computer system so we decided to go out to the pub for dinner and then put our feet up for the evening. On getting home, Laurence had just dropped off on the sofa when the phone shrilled out. He jumped back to consciousness like a puppet yanked up by the strings.

I am just about to curse his work, when I notice the intense tone of his voice. Laurence's dad has collapsed and the ambulance crew are at the bungalow giving him oxygen. Laurence has rushed over to transport his mum to his brother's for the night while his dad is in hospital.

A fist of panic hits my chest as I listen. What on earth will happen next?

THURSDAY 14TH AUGUST

Good news from the hospital as Laurence's dad is likely to be allowed home today. We find out that his collapse was due to simple heat stroke, at least partly brought on by his exhausting holiday. His mum has slept quite well at Laurence's brother's, but everything is uncertain and tense around us. It's as if that scary roller coaster we are on keeps developing a terrifying mechanical fault. I think we can just about keep ourselves on the rails – but if those around us keep tumbling, I don't even know if the wedding can take place.

As Chris has my car I'm effectively grounded. This is a good thing. In the morning I finish a pile of assignments that have been hanging around the house all week and tackle something that is way behind schedule – the white chocolate curls for my wedding cake. With some trepidation, I try to cool down the sun-hammered kitchen by stopping any cooking or other activity. As I melt the first batch of chocolate I'm concentrating so hard I feel like a scientist performing some bizarre lab experiment. The first batch doesn't look hopeful but I spread it on the marble slab with the wallpaper scraper. My first attempt is too tacky. Then, like magic, the chocolate curls actually form. Thank you, thank you! After four batches of chocolate I have a carton of white chocolate curls of varying standards in the freezer. Oh, and about 20 mouthfuls of gorgeous melted chocolate have winged their way to my greedy lips.

As for shopping, my only outlet is the village post office. I get another six pages of musical score photocopied (0.60p) to finish making the confetti cones and also get the Banns certificate (£27) photocopied to keep as a record (70p). Maybe I should stay at home more often?

FRIDAY 15TH AUGUST

Off to Laurence's parents and so relieved to see them at home, although his dad is still wobbly and his mum's wrist still looks as if it could be fractured. Next, off to Annie's Brides at 10.30am for my fitting. The dress is as lovely as ever, but there are two slight concerns:

Firstly, the bodice is still tight. I can't believe it. Never mind having the dress taken in, it's more a case of how many inches I can lose in the next 14 days.

Secondly, the bra I bought for the day isn't suitable as the lace shows. So off I went to Marks and Sparks *again*, this time to get a lower cup one with invisible plastic straps (£22).

DRESSED FOR SUCCESS

UNDERWEAR

The most important consideration in choosing your underwear is the impact it has on your dress.

- Bridal mags are full of extreme basques but forget frills and diamante edging if your dress is smooth or has its own boning. Go for smooth lycra or as little as you can possibly wear on the day.
- If your bra shows, consider 'Stickies' for invisible support *(£6)*, a backless bustiere *(about £30)* or attach invisible acrylic straps *(£6 per pack)*.
- If your dress, figure and budget allows, you could treat yourself to a once in a lifetime pair of totally frivolous knickers.
  Pink satin ribbon ties: £25
  ...or the infamous Pearl G-string: £130+

TIP: *Do have your mum or bridesmaid check your gown from all angles to ensure no annoying straps or fastenings spoil your dress.*

SATURDAY 16TH AUGUST

Wake up this morning and realise that it's two weeks today. I am so relieved that it is my horrible period today; if it were my wedding day I'd be in a real mess with stomach cramps and regular trips to the loo. I give a private thank you for all the modern medications that give women some choice about when these things happen.

It is wonderful to be able to stay at home today and do things quietly in our own space.

I start to sketch my ideas for the cake and visualise the arms of the 'S' shape metal stand covered in red satin ribbon and ivy. While Laurence is printing the Order of Service upstairs, I do my Blue Peter bit, making artificial ivy circles (thank goodness my sister warned me real ivy is poisonous) to fit around the three cakes using a coat hanger and florist's wire. I hold up the red paper cotton roses and decide that as few as three large blooms will be enough, set in a diagonal across each tier.

Catering For Success

Wedding Cake

There is a mouthwatering choice of cakes at every price and to suit every theme:

- Fun 'Saucy Bed' sugarcraft cake
  eg Jane Asher Party Cakes, serves 30: about £60
- An off-the-shelf three-tier cake you can decorate yourself
  Supermarket luxury fruit cake serves 75: about £70 including pillars
- A conventional three tier fruit cake with white icing, pillars and sugar flowers
  High street baker: £90-200
- Pavlova meringue tower dressed with edible flowers
  Specialist patissiere: £5 per serving
- Fairytale castle with icing turrets
  Specialist patissiere, serves 150: around £600
- For non-sweet tooths – tiers of delicious cheeses decorated with fruit and nuts
  Specialist provider, serves 150: from £125

  Silver-plated knife and server: about £50
  Cake stand hire (to elevate the cake): £5-20
  Porcelain cake top figurine: from £10-30

The non-speeches section is falling into shape now. Unfortunately Liz doesn't feel up to reading, after all her medical issues of the last few weeks. However Martin, our Accrington pal, has emailed a selection of his own work and Laurence and I have chosen two sensitive pieces. Behind the scenes, Laurence has also visited our friend Ed who will read a section on love from The Lay of the Last Minstrel. Finally, Laurence has tackled another major issue, which is visiting Jonathan to show him the Order of Service and our poems. Thankfully, he has approved it all.

The Order of Service design is so beautiful I want to have it framed after the wedding. In the corners are a lion (I assume that's Laurence, all grave and noble) and a griffin (think of a pouncing vulture with huge feet and wings caught in an hysterical mid-air flap, ie obviously me). The text is printed over the same design of gothic windows we used on our invitations. Each Order of Service is on a piece of A3 cream card that will be rolled up and held with gold cord I've bought from Abakhan (£15). He's used the same lion and griffin design on the menus, where the wines are also printed in gold. It is all very romantic and yet surreal, like an illustration from Alice in Wonderland.

The only part of the non-speeches still unresolved is the thank yous. Occasionally, I remember my prepared speech but won't get it out again as it makes me feel ill. I just don't want to disturb our new peace by discussing it, but someone will have to deliver it. Whenever I remember it I want to curl up and bury my head somewhere soft and very dark....

MONDAY 18TH AUGUST

A big day for us, as it's our last village hall visit. The hall looks rather dingy to me but Keith and Laurence seem quite happy with it all. At 2pm Leonie arrives and we have a frantic meeting in the kitchen. I confirm our final numbers: 70 people in the day and a further 23 in the evening. She loves the menu Laurence has designed and miraculously agrees to all my niggling concerns about the cake, the food presentation and even my latest brainwaves of hot chocolate sauce and mini-sparklers for the dessert. I also confide my heebie-jeebies about the bad weather forecast and the amount of cold food on the menu. Leonie agrees to increase the quantities of hot food, just in case we all need bowls of boiling soup to warm our rain soaked hands.

Team Management

Planning For Rain

The British weather means there is a one in three chance of rain every day. You must have a Plan D (for Deluge) against every important stage of your day:

- Find out what ideas your photographer has for a rainy day. Does he or she have plans to switch external shots back under cover, or a repertoire of fun shots in green wellies?

- Ensure you have lots of umbrellas on hand, including one large enough to adequately cover your dress.
- Does your open top car or carriage have a hood that can be raised in a shower?
- Can an awning be erected over a wedding arbour or other essential places you have earmarked for photographs?
- Is there heating at your venue? Do you know how to switch it on?
- What facilities do you have to increase the amount of hot drinks and food?

There's an unpleasant surprise when Leonie inspects the crockery. She takes one look and says it isn't adequate as the bowls are too small for soup or dessert. We agree that she will hire masses of large white restaurant-type crockery, along with heavy traditional cutlery. So this is yet another great unknown cost I've just lumped onto our budget.

Another disappointment is the proposed burgundy backdrop to cover the stage wall. Alan, from the village hall Committee, had thought it might be ready for our wedding but it won't be. So we now have a stage with two curtains that don't close and behind them an ancient bronze radiator and scrappy wall.

TUESDAY 19TH AUGUST

If you would have asked me about my fantasy of events just 10 days before the wedding, it would have been a soft focus image of me sauntering through florists and lingerie shops with my sisters, looking radiant and airily pondering whether baby rose buds or creamy freesias would look best in my gorgeously conditioned and radiant hair. Reality beckons:

9AM: *Chase wedding rings (without which we cannot be married) in a panic. Rings not ready. Tidy house, hoover carpets. Realise this is displacement activity and I should be ordering drinks. Go online and get distracted by guest emails. Chuck masses of water/lemonade/Aqua Libra in cyber shopping cart. Message flashes: Aqua Libra out of stock! Decide to shop like human being. Ring Chester Tesco: One bottle of Aqua Libra left. Ring Wrexham Tesco. No bottles of Aqua Libra left. Brain can no longer make sense of the Aqua Libra question. Postman knocks: half-Welsh letter eventually translated as speeding ticket. Three points and*

£60. Crime? 38 mph on dual carriageway. Panic over mind boggling pressure to change name on driving licence within 28 days. Grrrhhh! Phone! Keith: stag do for Laurence on Tuesday. Phone! Lorraine: 99 million bitsy issues. Gives me shopping list of items to buy and craft items to make. Laurence comes home to chaotic house mess and fiancee's chaotic head mess. Can't sit down as too agitated. Are Laurence's Oxford friends Nik, Marianne and Eleonor coming or not? We're both baffled but people need to know. Phone! Fran: When do we want greenery? Open parcel from old friend telling me she can no longer make it to the wedding. Crashing disappointment. Phone! Cousin Anne: Laurence asks what time we can visit Peter who is in a terrible state…

I have to stop it right there. Tears are rolling down my face. Pathetic, I know, but my whole emotional system has gone haywire. So much for blissful wedding planning…

Then on top of all this, I reach a major goal. I weigh myself and I'm actually 1lb *under* my target weight. It must have been water retention, reduced by all those gallons of tears…

FRIDAY 22ND AUGUST

Today I am so, so grateful to Laurence who has taken on the Taxi Problem and booked a minivan (not romantic but practical) to return any stragglers at the end of the night. We have picked up the rings (allelujah!) and they both look stunning. I keep running upstairs to peep at them in their cases. They are perfect symbols of the best part of this whole wedding thing – our actual marriage.

I've tried to counter my descent into manic depression (swinging from euphoric ecstasy to tearful collapse) by writing down my worst fears tonight. I used to consider myself quite a stable, placid sort of individual. Now, looking at the scrawl, maybe I actually am going bonkers?

DREAD LIST – ONE WEEK BEFORE WEDDING

- Guest(s) may get drunk, abusive – or even violent.
- I will look just pathetic.
- My ash blonde highlights will look like cobweb grey ringletted Miss Haversham.
- I will fall over while walking up the aisle and split my skirt.
- My bride's speech will give me a heart attack or, at the very least, a shaking, air gulping panic attack.
- Laurence will ad lib a totally unprepared speech and dry up in appalling silence/fall over drunk/make massively unfunny fall-flat jokes.
- The food will be unspeakably awful/be freezing/cause a food poisoning fiasco.
- It will rain non-stop leaving everyone wet, shivering and resentful.
- I will be physically ill and trudge through the day in a fevered daze.
- I will be mentally ill (no change there, then) and trudge through the day in a heavily sedated psychotic state.
- The band will be ridiculous and no one will dance.
- Gangs of rustic youths will steal all our alcohol or gate-crash and cause a violent rumpus.
- Everyone will sneer at our half-baked, home-crafted attempt at a wedding.

I suppose we could still cancel?

After all that writing therapy, I can barely face another sleepless, sheet twisting night. Gloomily, I clamber into bed.

"What's the matter, sweetheart?" Laurence opens his arms and I suddenly remember what all this is about. We're getting married. It's a miracle, not a nightmare. He gives me the sort of hug that makes my eyes smart and my throat burn.

"I'm so worried," I mumble. "We're spending so much money. Oh, I don't even know if there's any point to it all." I bury my head and snivel deep into his dressing gown.

"It's an expensive do," he commiserates. "I must give you some more cash. I'll give you another £500 in the morning. Will that do?" I nod deep into his chest. "And I suppose I should pay for the photography when the bill comes in."

Even in the midst of turmoil my head is doing calculations. Five hundred pounds plus the £685 for photography – that's £1,185. Not bad. Put that besides my Slosh Account and everyone else's contributions and we're getting close to target. In fact, it's fantastic.

Only it doesn't make me feel fantastic. I feel like saying, forget it. It's only money after all. Is it worth it? That's my point. All the bother, the work, the anxiety. The stress that's sapping me, that's making me feel sick, the mixture of dread and excitement about the bride's speech, for example...

"The thank yous are killing me," I confess. "It's a whole side of A4. Oh God, it's going to ruin my whole wedding day," I bleat, choking back the tears.

"Tell me what it is again?"

Hasn't he been listening? I feel like he could already have grounds for divorce due to my excessive wittering about these bloody thank yous.

"It's just the bit where someone has to say thanks to Lorraine and Keith and everyone who's helped and turned up. I've got bouquets ordered. Only I'm so scared of having to stand up and say it."

"It's all right," he says, shaking his head and smiling at my outburst. "Just write it out for me. I'll do it. Now come here, you …" I sleep like a baby. What a hero. At last I can enjoy my wedding day again.

SATURDAY 23RD AUGUST

Promptly, Laurence writes me another cheque for £500. Now, at the eleventh hour I can finally see his perspective on money. In fact, I'd say that without him acting as a brake on the whole proceedings this wedding could easily have cost us double what has been spent. As I bank the cheque I grudgingly admire his 'careful' attitude. Whatever happens, we have managed to keep our budget to less than half the average spend on a wedding. And it's only thanks to him. *And* he's paid off half our mortgage. *And* he's going to stand up and deliver my bride's speech. Rather guiltily, I remember the hundreds I've been spending recently on – what? Flowers, candles, chocolates and plantpots. Hmph!

Together, we also decide that Nik and co will probably arrive after all, so I email and post the final numbers to everyone who could possibly care. I've also found a reader to replace Liz in my work colleague Gwen, so I email her a few possible readings.

Once the fierce sun starts to sink after dinner, we go out for a walk through the twilit lanes. Reaching Shordley, Laurence shows me the farm he lived on as a boy. We clamber along sunken paths to an Anglo-Saxon moat and ancient manor house where bats flicker through the purple skies. Foxes bark and the black silhouettes of trees whisper around us. Laurence tells me about the precious childhood he lost when he had to spend more than a year in hospital and came out to find his family had moved from his beloved farmhouse. But now, he tells me, he has found me and I'm so precious to him. Coming home we spend a quiet evening tying up the Orders of Service with gold cord and piling them in our be-ribboned wicker hamper. I am so contented and happy.

Sunday 24th August

Everything feels so good this morning for both of us. As I gather my final harvest of rose petals for confetti, the church bells ring out across the village and we both realise that this time next week we will be married. The trug of confetti is now full and I've decorated it with white satin ribbons. We eat breakfast and potter around outside and all the omens feel so good this morning.

Tuesday 26th August

I check the weather forecast for Saturday again and it is definitely going to rain. This is so hateful. All my hard work is going to waste and the whole wedding will be a ghastly damp squib. I have to keep getting the rings out to remind myself about the married bit and try to forget the washed out wedding.

Later, I'm cheered by picking up my dress and smuggling it upstairs while Laurence isn't around. Mmm, it still looks so gorgeous. I've just dropped Chris and Laurence at their stag night where Laurence announced that he's not going to drink much at all. A whole night on my own – how exciting! Firstly, I time myself putting on my haul of delicious new make-up while jotting down the details. This takes an unbelievable 1½ hours to put on, as I'm taking massive care with every brushstroke. Next I try on my underwear, jewellery and finally… the dress. I look in the mirror and – I actually look rather nice. Not a hint of Miss Haversham!

Finally, after midnight, Keith rings for me to go and collect them in the car. Laurence is very drunk, he laughs. I shake my head in disbelief. What is he like?

The fun starts on the way home. Chris is as cheery and amiable as he always is when a bit tiddly. Laurence feels violently ill.

"Shtop the car," he cries, as we leave Chester. I pull over into a benighted lay-by. He stumbles out and grasps a fence. A herd of young calves stare back at him. Chris and I sit in the car, giggling. The calves are creeping closer to my doubled up fiancé. His head is hanging upside down over the fence.

"Laurence," I call out. "You're going to get cow dribble on your head."

"All wight now." Laurence slumps back into the passenger car. "Never dwinking again," he mumbles. Chris is in fits of laughter in the back.

"Shtop the car." Again I slow down but this time we're on a single track road. "Ahm gonna be shick," he moans. I stop, regardless of any traffic.

"Don't fall in a ditch," I cry as he shambles into the verge. Soon he's back again, reportedly, "All wight". Five times we stop.

Five times I manage a few hundred yards before he threatens to vomit all over the inside of my car. It takes nearly an hour to get home.

Gratefully I roll him into bed and the inevitable jet engine drone starts up beside me. Finally, I get to sleep, dreaming of shiny satin shoes and glittery eye shadows. Mmm, what a lovely girly evening I've had. Then I hear the extractor starting up in the en suite bathroom. It is 2am and Laurence is in there, groaning into the loo bowl. He hangs there for the next hour, flushing the loo loudly every five minutes and muttering to himself.

But he is wonderful. In the morning he disinfects the loo and cleans the en suite from floor to ceiling. I've just got to marry this man.

Wednesday 27th August

The action is hotting up today as it's my pampering day and the rehearsal this evening. First of all, I gratefully zoom off to 'Essence of Beauty' for a bit of a rest. Thank goodness I booked this last month after endless prevarication over the cost. When I finally rang, almost all of August was booked and I'm lucky to find a free session. First off is a Thalgo O2 Facial (divine cold and warm sensations, sensual scents and delicious massage) followed by honeymoon pedicure (fun fuschia nail polish on toes) and finally, a full body exfoliation and Guinol tan. The damage is £110 but I do feel pretty and glowing after all that lying around and rubbing of expensive creams into my body. Lovely.

THE PURSUIT OF BRIDAL BEAUTY

PAMPERING

A pampering session is as much about allowing yourself precious time and space as taking a short cut to a smooth complexion, light tan and perfect nails:
Three-night Health Spa break: around £400

High Street Beauty Salon:
Bridal package – facial, brow shape, lash tint, make-up, Thalgo wrap, manicure, pedicure: about £120
Wedding make-up including trial: about £35
Aromatherapy massage: £32
Nail extensions: about £30
Thalgo facial: about £30
Full body exfoliation and artificial tan: £25

There is barely time to grab some food and handfuls of papers before we dash off to the wedding rehearsal. Jonathan guides us through the ceremony from my first walk up to the church doors, procession down the aisle with Nicola, to arrival at the altar. Dad has an opportunity to run through his musical accompaniment and I read the poem alongside him, in place of Marijke. The music he has written for me is a beautiful, rippling composition. I am very touched by this and so proud of him. Fran also has a chance to recite her poem and Jonathan subtly coaches us all in every aspect, from projecting voices to standing in the right places. Finally, he suggests that Laurence and I stay behind to practice our vows while everyone else goes home. As he leaves, Dad thrusts a gift into my hands from his partner, Olivia. It's a crystal cake knife and server that will look beautiful as we cut the cake.

Alone with Jonathan in the increasing gloom of the high-vaulted church, we practise the simple words that will marry us. Occasionally, he tells us little asides that he knows will interest us – that plighting our 'troth' means giving our 'true oath', and that when we approach the high altar this symbolises our journey through life together. Twice during the ceremony we will have to kneel; a rather nerve wracking prospect in my tight skirt and train. I find the ceremony thrilling, fearful and yet, with Jonathan guiding us, wonderfully reassuring. He assures that we have only to repeat the words after him and we will be married.

Thursday 28th August

It's raining and it's cold. It's also 10am at the village hall and the hard labour ahead of me makes me want to curl up and go back to sleep. I feel so dispirited that I'm reminded of a long trek I once took into the Spanish Mountains with Laurence. At the end of six hours tough walking we got lost. Finally, stumbling through the forest, virtually hallucinating the prospect of a hot bath and bed, we glimpsed our Parador hotel perched high above us on a wooded ridge. By some strange optical illusion it looked close enough to reach out and grasp with our hands, but in reality it was countless precipitous miles ahead up rapidly darkening paths. Somehow, that day, I had mustered my inner strength to reach safety by nightfall. That's how I feel today, shivering in the dingy hall as the rain whips against the windows. Exhausted, disappointed and rather scared.

"I must have been mentally ill not to book a hotel."

"We-ell," is all Lorraine says. She's huffing at the state of the walls, dragging out trestle tables to spread her Victorian wallpaper. I do my best to titivate the loos, setting up draped little tables of hand creams, soaps and fresh towels. Unfortunately, I can't ignore

the real pit of hell forever – the hall entrance. It is filthy. Furry cobwebs hang in black curtains. Even with rubber gloves, hot water and disinfectant, all I seem to do is transfer black water from one spot to another. I fantasise about turning up at some highly polished hotel just like any other bride, surrounded by staff eager to wait on me, and the chance just to lie back polishing my nails in a bubbling Jacuzzi. Why on earth was I so stupid? And there's poor Lorraine to think of, slaving away with her panels. It's noon and she's only managed to put up two. We could be here till midnight.

It's a relief to get out of the place and trundle off to Chester to pick up the cake stand and a sandwich lunch. At least Laurence has arrived by the afternoon and Chris proves invaluable transporting car loads of drink and decorations. No one else turns up. This isn't what The Plan said would happen...

Debenhams are scheduled to drop off our gifts after 4pm but I feel guilty leaving the others to go home at 5pm. As I leave, the wallpaper is looking good and Laurence has got a few of his exhibition panels ready. But it still looks awful. Cold. Empty. Like some crazy person's idea of a wedding venue. And it's still sheeting down with rain.

At home a card through the door tells me I've missed the Debenham's van. This is terrible. Our guests have gone to the immense expense and trouble of buying us gifts and we haven't even made proper arrangements to take delivery. All day tears have been hot behind my eyes and now I'm alone I sink my head into my hands. This is feeling like a nightmare – only its real, it's happening, and it's my wedding.

I ring the driver and miraculously, he agrees to drive over at 6pm – that man is a star. There's just the cake to assemble tonight.

Then I can get off to bed and things can only get better...

Getting Organised

Thank You Cards

A note of appreciation should be sent to everyone who sends a gift or helps out in any way – immediately after the wedding, if not before:

- It is a nice gesture (and good etiquette) to write cards by hand and not simply send a printed message.
- Mention the particular gift and how you will be using and enjoying it.
- If money was sent, or vouchers, describe how you intend to spend it.
- If writing after the wedding, describe any particular recollections you have about the gift giver from the day.

Blank thank you cards – high street: 20 cards about £8
Printed thank you cards: £50-100 for 100 cards

9PM: Disaster. The others are watching a film in the living room but I'm still here in the kitchen. The middle cake tier now has sticky ganache all over it and I'm starting to stick on the white chocolate curls. But as I apply them, they are breaking in my hands. I get another freezer box out. Even worse. Almost all of them just shatter on contact, like some unearthed treasure turning to dust. I realise, with what feels like a mild heart attack, that the summer's heat has irrevocably damaged the chocolate. I don't have anything like enough curls to cover the cake.

Laurence pops his head around the door. "Come and watch the film."

"I can't." I'm trying to control my panic. There are shreds of white chocolate everywhere. It could look like a romantic Christmas scene. Only this is my wedding cake falling like snow all over the kitchen worktops and floor.

Half an hour later, he's back. "Come and sit down."

My bottom lip is wobbling. I'm having serious co-ordination problems now. It's as if my hands are turning everything I touch into white chocolate dust.

"I can't." But the subtext is there in my reproachful glare. I should have bought a cake, it says. You *made me* suffer like this. As if the kitchen isn't enough of a bomb site I push past him to get more cream out of the fridge and it slips through my fingers and splurges all over the floor. I can't see for tears as he gets bundles of kitchen towels out and kneels to mop it up.

"Do it in the morning." He grabs my arm. "Go up to bed. Now."

But it's not in The Plan, I want to bleat. The Plan says the cake is finished tonight and I'm down at the hall co-ordinating all the deliveries tomorrow. That's The Plan. Very slowly, my brain begins to cogitate. I've only got one single bag of white chocolate left to make one last batch of curls. Even I can see I'm in no fit state to work on the cake tonight. So I start to scrape up the huge mess of chocolate from my worktops, my sink, my cooker, my chairs, my apron, my hair...

FRIDAY 29TH AUGUST

3AM: I'm so, so worried about the cake. I'm punch drunk with this nightmare of pressure. And I'm so tired. Had an utterly dreadful sleep, waking bolt upright at 1.40am. What if the last batch of chocolate doesn't curl? What if I can only finish two tiers of the cake? It will look so stupid half covered. I feel sick, physically and mentally. Thankfully Chris is staying over with my mum, so I can creep to the spare bedroom to try to read myself to sleep. That doesn't work. I try listening to the World Service. Doesn't work. Counting backwards. Doesn't work. Relaxation tape. Doesn't work. Feel like Dr Jekyll and Mrs Hyde, having to physically restrain myself from going downstairs and trying to finish the cake. The cruellest blow is that I know this is not how my last day before the wedding should be spent. It's all my own fault. I've completely ruined my own wedding. I could howl up to the moon with misery.

10AM: Almost miraculously brighter this morning after sleeping from 3.30am to 7am. Lorraine went off early to tackle the hall. None of us slept well. The cockerel woke her at 4am and like me, she had a head full of To Dos and Don't Forgets. I do wonder if the wedding will be like childbirth – with only memories of the joyful climax and total amnesia about the agony and suffering? But how could we ever forget?

Now that I'm alone I steel myself for the last assault on the chocolate mountain. I have only 900g of couverture chocolate left for the huge bottom tiers. What if it doesn't work? I decide that there must be some Aztec god of chocolate somewhere in the heavens and offer up a prayer to that long neglected deity. I begin to melt and spread my last, my most precious bag.

I am rewarded by huge, creamy, cigar-thick curls of chocolate that would not look out of place in a Jane Asher Cake Extravaganza. There are enough to cover the whole cake. Perfecto.

NOON: At last I can face breakfast. I sit out in the damp garden to enjoy a low-carb plate of sausages, bacon and buttered linseed bread. Just as I return to the kitchen to finish the final tier, Chris arrives home. I feel almost human again as he chats away, totally oblivious to his mother's near breakdown. Then, as I complete the bottom tier of the cake with a whole stockade of solid fingers of chocolate my heartbeat seems to slow back to a steady normal rate. It looks fabulous.

1.30PM: We drive through the rain to the hall. The plastic shopping boxes left behind by Tesco Home Delivery prove invaluable to transport all three tiers of the cake down to the hall, carefully bolstered by towels. It works. Chris and I lift the cake into the village hall fridge and all three tiers are in pristine condition. Phew…

Beyond, an incredible surprise awaits me. The hall is transformed. The grotty entrance is now a gauzy, flower draped anteroom. The main room itself is full of furniture – 70 elegant gold chairs with brocaded burgundy seats and seven huge round tables. And here is Keith, bursting with energy, always on the move, twitching and longing to act; happiest up a ladder, fixing, solving and sorting. He's rigged up the four giant hanging baskets to the beams on chains – for practical genius, we couldn't have found a better best man. His mum Fran, a former nursing sister, is working like a Trojan too, sorting through masses of greenery, ivies and herbs to decorate the hall. I can't believe how different everything is. Lorraine has finished the wallpaper panels and is swagging the burgundy curtains above each window.

I get a new lease of life and after serving up lunch I lay the ivory linen on the tables. Lorraine's huge iron candelabras look like props from a gothic film as I load them with dozens of ivory tapering candles. Yvonne and Liz don't arrive but later, Laurence's cousin Dawn and friend Angela turn up with Dawn's baby, Thomas. Dawn lays the favours, bubbles, tealights, chocolates and place cards on the tables. Meanwhile, Lorraine produces the hand painted table plan and displays it on a quaint wooden easel, garlanded with ivy.

Sue, our florist is the next to pop in and tell us she has finished the church flowers. Laurence's exhibition now looks spectacular, suspended from the oak dividers normally covered in playgroup art, spreading in two wings on either side of the entrance. He has one section displaying his amazing artwork, combining photography and poetry. On the other side are enlarged family photographs, some reaching back to the 1860s. Taking a long look at the hall it does look amazing. Lorraine and Keith have suspended panels of rich plum brocade above the stage to cover the radiator and also staple gunned red velvet to the front of the stage. The ingenuity of it all is extraordinary.

4.30PM*:* The caterers arrive – en masse. They compliment us on the hall and get down to work with cool professionalism: folding napkins, moving tables, laying cutlery and unloading mysterious boxes into the kitchen. At this moment, I feel all my remaining worry drift heavenwards and pop, like the bubbles we test from our bubble guns. Lorraine wants to get away now to meet her husband Nick and son Alexander at their hotel. "It's over to the professionals now," we say, as they take over the hall that is at last – stylishly and elegantly – finished.

Outside, rainstorms continue but a new mood of accomplishment refreshes the air. After a lavender scented bath I wash and dry my hair ready for the hairdressers. Laurence and I are shattered and go up to bed with aching limbs. Then, just as I think my tasks are finally over, he produces his folder of notes for the non-speeches. He reads through the poems and even the thank yous I've written out for him and I mumble my approval from the depths of the duvet. He's even collected together spares of everyone else's poems, including Martin's. I've had an email from our Accrington pal requesting a copy of the poem so earlier tonight I'd searched the internet and forwarded a copy to him. Laurence tells me that he, too, has had a last minute request for a tie from him and given him further instructions on finding the poem himself. Exhausted as we are, we get up again, find a tie and pack it away in the ceremony box. Surely there can't be anything else?

Then, just as we are nodding off, there's a knock at the door. It's Chris. "They've just given the weather forecast for Chester Races," he says excitedly through a gap in the door. "Sunshine!" Snuggling up to Laurence I feel good. I have no worries left at all. The cake is ready in the fridge. The hall has been transformed. And we're getting married in the morning.

TIME STOPS

7.20AM: It must have been the lavender fizz balls in my bath, or maybe just the sense of so much accomplished but I wake from a blissful sleep to hear the phone ringing downstairs. The sun is shining! The sky is blue! Yet surely this can't last. Laurence wakes beside me and we smile into each other's eyes, so pleased that we went against tradition and stayed the night together. Whenever we had been restless in the night we held hands or just curled around each other. It makes me feel we are embarking on this great day as a strong partnership – together.

Nipping downstairs, I find a message from our friend Carole in Egypt, who rang to wish us well. On the doormat lies a pile of pastel envelopes to add to our mountain of presents and cards delivered last night. The atmosphere starts to build as I have a quiet moment alone in the conservatory. The sun filled room feels charged with sparkling energy. It's our wedding day at last! Dressing, I remember Clare's advice to wear a front-opening top so I won't mess up my hair. Driving through the lanes to Farndon the sky is as blue as Wedgewood pottery and the sun shines hot through the windscreen. Unbelievable.

10AM: Farndon looks so beautiful as I arrive over the old stone bridge where a cluster of black and white buildings perch on the

hillside. Clare supplies constant good humoured chat and hot tea as she starts to curl my hair with sizzling tongs. I show her the picture I've chosen and after placing my tiara she begins to roll barrel curls just behind it, letting a cascade of ringlets fall in a lovely tangle. Finally, she sets diamond pins and hair springs into the curls.

Hilary and Helen are also having their hair fixed and it really is quite funny to see little Helen with a head full of curlers under a hair drier reading a copy of 'Hello!' I've remembered my camera and we take a couple of snaps as we're getting ready.

11.20AM: Arrive home to find Laurence casually chatting to Hilary's husband, Ron, in the conservatory. After a rapid exchange about the glorious weather, Laurence agrees to take some more of our own garden furniture over to the hall as he's going to make some last minute checks. As he leaves with Chris I have the house to myself for a few precious minutes. I calculate that if my sister is coming in the bridal car at 1.45pm that doesn't leave me very long to get ready.

Realising I'll be drinking but not eating until about 5pm, I grab a sandwich, although I'm not at all hungry. Then the phone rings and it's Keith. Everything is fine, he reassures me, but our friend from Accrington has arrived. Where are the tie and the poem? Aaargh! The tie, I assure him, is in the ceremony box, and as for the poem (that I emailed him last night and that Laurence has given him instructions on finding on the net himself), there are stacks of copies of that in Laurence's folder *and* in the ceremony box. Honestly, I could dictate the whole thing word for word from memory over the phone myself. If it wasn't my actual wedding day...

Beating a hasty retreat, I dash upstairs and start to pack. As well as my large overnight bag to transport my train, I'm taking a cream pashmina in case it's cold. All that I can realistically fit into the ivory drawstring bag is my lipgloss, compact, concealer, cotton buds and hairgrips. I put my engagement ring on my right hand and look for a moment at my bare wedding finger. Soon to be married, I think, excitedly.

One absolute blessing is my written list of wedding make-up; in my euphoria, I can't even remember what eye shadow I had finally chosen. About halfway through my make-up, Laurence and Chris both arrive home, shower and rapidly dress. The process seems straightforward, except for help tying ties and popping in cuff links. They both look so smart and elegant I only hope my dress will stand comparison. Kissing Laurence goodbye, I remind him that I will see him next at the altar. By now my nerves are fluttering like confetti in a wind tunnel!

1.30PM: Ding Dong! Lorraine, Nick and Alexander arrive early, all looking very stylish. While I finish getting ready they decorate the car with satin ribbons.

Getting Organised

Transport

Traditionally, formal transport is laid on to take the bride and giver away to the ceremony, often followed by a second car or carriage with the bridesmaids and bride's mother. The possibilities for making a grand entrance are endless:

A vintage car, limousine or sports car with chauffeur: from £200-700 per car

Helicopters or hot air balloons (if there is a landing place): Private

charters begin from £200 for a balloon and £450 for a helicopter
A horse drawn carriage: from £450
A mode of transport unique to you and your interests, from a tractor to motorbike, barge or boat

TIP: *As with every other wedding item, think carefully about saving your budget by begging or borrowing appropriate transport.*

Upstairs I finish my make-up and even Lorraine comments on how good it looks. With Lorraine's help I put on my great-grandmother's cameo necklace (something old) and my underwear (something new), my dress (something borrowed) and garter (something blue). Finally, I slip on my shoes in which I've sellotaped a lucky sixpence supplied by Keith (intended to bring me wealth, no less). Finally, we hook up the train and Lorraine pronounces the dress gorgeous.

Ding Dong! Hearing Marijke, her partner David and friend Julia arrive downstairs, I carefully pick up my train by its finger loop and step down the stairs feeling like a million dollars. Popping open a few bottles of champagne, we chat excitedly while I have a single glass to calm my nerves. The flowers have arrived and my bouquet is a Victorian fantasy of pink roses studded with pearls, linoleum berries, ferns and white rosebuds. Lorraine shows me how to hold it; almost horizontal with the stalks against my stomach so a trail of ferns falls downwards in a spray.

2.15PM: Ring, Ring! Phone call from Laurence: have the bridesmaid's flowers arrived here? No. They should be at the church. I manage to find the florist's phone number in my file and hurriedly give it to him.

2.30PM: All of a sudden, it's time to leave. After a few photos we climb into the car and I fold my train across my knees. Then, despite the glamorous possibilities, we leave the roof up as otherwise my ringlets will simply blow out in the breeze. As we drive through the lanes I tell the others about all the times I have imagined this journey. Now, the sun is shining and my whole body is tingling with excitement. As we swing down the lane into the village I feel an overpowering joy to be alive at this moment.

The Wedding Service

Countdown At The Church

On the morning of the wedding every member of the bridal party should have a clear idea of the timetable and the part they play in it:

Minus 2 hours	Bride and wedding party dress and get ready Best man takes rings and any necessary money or documents Receipt and distribution of flowers
Minus 40 minutes	Ushers arrive at church with buttonholes and service sheets Photographer arrives
Minus 30 minutes	Minister and organist arrive Guests begin to arrive
Minus 20 minutes	Groom and best man arrive Photographs of groom and best man at church Church fees paid if not already done so
Minus 10 minutes	Bride's mother and bridesmaids arrive and wait in the porch

Minus 5 minutes	Bride arrives and photographs taken
Minus 2 minutes	Minister greets bride at the porch
	Bride's mother takes up her seat
Minus 1 minute	Minister returns to the altar
	Groom and best man stand to the right of the chancel steps
	Organist begins processional music
	Congregation stands
Wedding Service	Bride and attendants walk slowly along the aisle

Pulling up at the towering gilded gates I can see a few members of the public waiting on the lane and a mass of friends and families gathered outside the church, mingling in an impressionist blur of pinks, blues and lilacs. Lorraine says, "Look. They are all here for you," and I feel amazed. It looks like a proper wedding – something I've had my doubts about over the last few days. John, our photographer, quickly sets up his camera and takes a couple of shots as I get out of the car. The powerful sun magnifies the vivid velvet green of the lawns and ochre Gothic church. At the entrance I can see Jonathan looking magnificent in a gold and green surplice.

Above me the church bell tolls three o'clock. Picking up my train, I take Chris's arm and get my first close view of the bridesmaids. The flowers clearly arrived without mishap as the circlets of white flowers in their long curls could grace Pre-Raphaelite maidens and the ribboned pomanders in their hands match perfectly. After Jonathan has greeted us, he and the rest of our guests disappear inside and Chris and I face the two massive solid wooden doors alone. My heart thumps against my boned bodice as we face the doors and wait. I feel a peculiar mix of emotions as we stand together – somewhere between ringing the doorbell outside a wonderful party and being a child sitting in a carriage outside the wooden doors of a ghost train.

From within I hear the organ strike up Vivaldi's 'Primavera' and slowly the twin doors creak apart. Taking slow and careful steps I walk inside the shadowy vastness of the church and feel the whole congregation straining towards me to catch a glimpse. Thankfully, ever practical Fran is there to fix a loose strap inside my dress before we turn towards the aisle. Beneath my feet I see the ancient black and white chequerboard tiles, while on either side of me I get my first view of the pink and white flower sprays on the pew ends. Faces peer at us and I feel so happy that at last this moment has come and all our guests have assembled.

At the head of the aisle I see Laurence glancing round at me, looking so smart in his blue morning coat. I can't wait to grasp his hand but first I have to negotiate giving my huge bouquet to my mum who is sitting in the front pew. Finally taking Laurence's hand, we smile at each other and I feel a great wave of relief that we have got this far without mishap. Jonathan now beams at us as he welcomes our guests to our long awaited wedding.

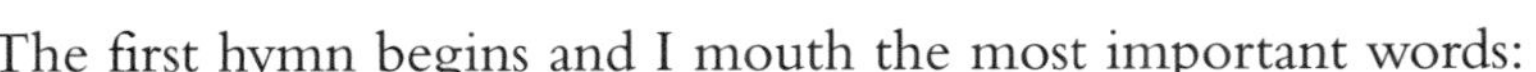

The first hymn begins and I mouth the most important words:

> *'Riches I heed not, nor man's empty praise*
> *Be thou mine inheritance now and always…'*

At the core of my bubbling excitement I am aware of all my secret hopes converging upon this public moment. When Jonathan asks, "Who gives this woman to be married to this man?" Chris replies in a loud voice, "I do!" Next, we get in a tangle of hands as Chris has to pass my right hand into Laurence's right hand, but each time we get muddled Jonathan unobtrusively guides us. One intimate touch is that our minister doesn't use our full names, just our Christian names. When Laurence repeats his vows after Jonathan, I feel so proud of him and want to concentrate on hearing every precious syllable. Time seems to stop as he repeats my name and promises to love, honour and cherish me. This is the high point of my life. Ever since I was a child there have been moments when I have wondered if I would ever meet the man destined for me. I try to focus on that uncertainty and sadness and utterly live in this wonderful moment of fulfilment as Laurence vows he will love me forever. Then it is my turn. I do my best and like Laurence, don't stumble. When called upon, Keith produces the rings and places them on the prayer book. It is a thrilling moment when Laurence slips the circle of gold onto my finger and I slip his ring onto his. Then Jonathan holds our hands up with his and proclaims "What God has bound together, let no man put asunder." The church seems to echo at his words and I know that we must both always resist temptation and, as our 'troth' signifies, honour our true-oath before God.

For the readings, we sit at the side of the chancel steps on two carved chairs that resemble thrones. Clasping hands, we watch as my dad plays the piano, producing a rippling theme that perfectly evokes this romantic occasion. After all our difficulties over the years, this again seems symbolic of our reconciliation and my wanting to let him know how much I admire his talent. Meanwhile, Marijke climbs to the carved pulpit, looking stunning in a lilac suit and cloche hat, and reads her poem beautifully to the piano accompaniment. Fran then strides forward and reads Shelley's 'Love's Philosophy' in a loud, ringing voice that makes me so proud of her confidence. After planning all these small events so carefully, it is mildly surprising to watch them unfold and not go disastrously wrong.

The Wedding Service

Civil Ceremonies

A civil ceremony, whether at a Registry Office or Approved Premises, differs from a church wedding in a number of ways:

- A civil wedding can be given unique touches such as personally written vows but must not include any religious references such as hymns, religious readings, prayers or spiritual music.
- The whole ceremony takes between 10 and 20 minutes at a Registry Office. At some Registry Offices there may be as many as three weddings per hour on a Saturday.
- Most Marriage Rooms at Registry Offices hold about 30 people and opportunities for flowers, decorations and music may be limited.
- Approved Premises often allow for a much more personalised wedding service with the greatest amount of flexibility of wording and expression. You can often book as long a service as you wish, and can design a highly personalised service with vows, music and readings to suit you.
- Approved premises will often give you a fairly free rein over decorations. Many, for example, will allow you to marry by candlelight.
- Your vows can be chosen from different versions, or you can write your own vows with the Registrar's prior approval.

Next, Jonathan mounts the pulpit. He talks about the Marriage at Canaan and the spirit of sharing on that day of the first miracle. He also tells us about a wedding he has recently seen in Crete and that the couple had worn crowns – stopping to point out that I, too, am wearing a kind of crown today. Sharing and togetherness are his theme as he slips in a literary quote from A A Milne. This beautifully personal short sermon helps me appreciate how important the celebrant of a wedding is in setting the tone for our day.

Standing again for our last hymn, 'Jerusalem', we can hear the choir and our congregation's voices swell. Yet before me I can see the embroidered kneeler and know that it is time to start thinking about kneeling in an elegant and ladylike fashion without tumbling over or splitting my dress. When the moment comes, Laurence helps me down as instructed at the rehearsal, and I clutch the wooden tracery to keep myself steady. Above us, Jonathan intones the prayers and blessings upon all of us.

Next, we must walk together towards the High Altar for our final blessing. Carefully getting up from my kneeler, I walk hand in hand with Laurence towards the towering gold carvings and altar. I feel we are leaving our family and friends and approaching the most sacred part of the church where every item of elaborate gold and covering of thick embroidery has a profound meaning. Beside us lies the massive entombed figure of Duke Hugh Lupus, lying supine in creamy marble. The air is thick with rites of birth, love and death. At the high altar we kneel again and receive God's blessing. It is a deeply mystical moment that I feel privileged to experience.

As the religious service ends we file into the Grosvenor chapel to sign the register. We are married. Our parents and the bridal party meet with us and the solemn atmosphere is lifted by family kisses and congratulations. While our two fathers sign as witnesses, our photographer begins to set up. Turning to Nicola, my youngest bridesmaid, I asked her how she enjoyed the service. "It was a little bit boring," she declares. Well, out of the mouths of babes, as they say, comes wisdom...

I am hardly bored, as I have to concentrate on signing the register in my old name, in full, in joined up writing. Given the emotion of the moment, that is quite enough for me to concentrate on.

Once the register is signed, Laurence and I process along the aisle among our well-wishers. As the organ strikes up and the church bells begin pealing, great surges of excitement make my breath tremble. After all the strain of the last few weeks I can barely feel the ground beneath my satin shoes as our friends and family beam at us. Emerging into the golden sunlight everyone gathers to congratulate us. The bright sun gilds the whole village, as if it too were dressed to match our wedding theme of gold and ivory. Everywhere, cameras click and we grin like two celebrities at a premiere. On cue, Fran organises my two nephews to fire up their bubble guns and suddenly the air is a hail of iridescent bubbles popping and dancing around us. Everyone laughs and chatters as we make our way to the green lawns at the side of the church. Thankfully, John organises all the photography from his schedule and for 15 minutes or so we jostle and line up in the sunshine until our faces begin to ache from smiling. Everyone looks so stylish – Auntie Sheila a picture in fuschia and my new mum-in-law so elegant in pink and cream.

OUR PHOTOGRAPHY LIST

- The Church and village hall
- Groom alone
- Groom with his brothers
- Groom with his parents
- Groom, best man and ushers
- Bridesmaids
- Bride and giver away
- Bride and bridesmaids
- Bride and bridal party and car
- Signing the register
- Bride and groom in the aisle
- Bride and groom with bubbles
- Bride and groom with confetti
- Everyone all together
- Bride with sisters
- Bride and groom with bride's family
- Bride and groom with groom's family
- Bride and room with friends
- Portraits by the Monument or River

In the hall:

- The cake
- Cutting the cake
- The toast
- All afternoon and at Ceilidh – informal reportage pictures

As guests drift away in groups, we have an opportunity to share a few words together.

"Isn't it wonderful," I gush to Laurence. He looks so happy, too, as he agrees that it was a wonderful ceremony. He keeps touching his wedding ring and raising his finger to flex and admire it on his hand. I notice that when we approach people we are simply the Bride and Groom. They congratulate us but don't expect a real conversation, thank goodness. Beyond saying, "Lovely to see you," and "How are you?" I'm experiencing all of this as a kind of out of body experience. Intelligent conversation is definitely not within my grasp.

Reaching the high ornamental gates we pause while the ushers hand out the rose petals. When the confetti flies into the air at a shout from John, I'm afraid we both laugh so hard at the huge shower that afterwards the photos show us with our faces screwed up looking very strange.

4.30PM: Our last photo call at the Rectory is a delightful shot of myself, Laurence and Jonathan while wolfhound Lupus pokes his hairy head through the gate. As time is passing, we saunter down the wide lane towards the river and the village hall. Our Order of Service includes a brief Order of the Day that gives our guests an idea of timings and this is now directing them towards the lawn for drinks:

ORDER OF THE DAY

Approximate Times	
Wedding ceremony	3pm
Photographs and drinks	4pm
Celebration meal (village hall)	5pm
Cake cutting and toasts	6.30pm
Arrival of evening guests	7.30pm

Ceilidh with 'Devil's Fire'	8pm
Interval and refreshments	9.15pm
'Devil's Fire' – second set	9.45pm
Taxis and farewells	11pm

Outside the village hall everything is perfect. The tables are set with their green cloths, pink candle lamps and cyclamen pots. The jewel coloured candles have been strung on the fence and in the trees. Our guests look happy and relaxed as waitresses pass between them with silver trays of sparkling wine and buck's fizz. Another round of photographs commences, this time fun shots of friends and children as we crowd together on the lawn, basking in the warm rays of the summer sun. All around us our guests cluster in webs of friendship and kinship; chattering and laughing, greeting old acquaintances and renewing old bonds.

As I kneel between my two bridesmaids for a photograph, Nicola turns her grave grey eyes on me again. What will her next startlingly honest pronouncement be? "I have to say, Laura," she begins solemnly, "you look extra, extra beautiful today." Well, out of the mouths of babes, as I said…

5PM: Walking into the hall through the pink voile drapes I secretly consider what I know lies beneath the gauzy swagging – broken electricity boxes, gouged holes, old blu-tack and rusty nails. Then before me spreads the whole room transformed like Cinderella's pumpkin. Vivid pink baskets of mossy flowers hang on ivy chains from the ceiling beams, creamy linen cloths are laid with sparkling glassware and silver, and at the centre of each table stands a tall glass vase of pink water topped with a spray of delicate flowers and foliage held in pearl studded net. Before us stands the pretty easel displaying Lorraine's hand painted table plan. Laurence's exhibition stands on either side, immediately attracting great huddles of interested guests.

My train has a habit of getting under people's feet; after the last ripping sensation I know it's time to remove it. Up in the hall's attic, I take a moment to breathe the dusty air and try to gulp down this perfect day with every part of my senses. Folding the train away in my bag, I pelt downstairs unencumbered and take up my place for our meal.

Beside us sits my cake on its stand. Thanks to Leonie, it is even better than I had ever hoped it would be. Approaching it, the luxurious scent of real chocolate rises, like the rich aroma in a continental *chocalatier.* It stands in three huge layers like solid tiered hatboxes covered in fingers of white chocolate caraque. The topping of summer fruits is stunning: fat scarlet strawberries, puckered raspberries and trails of redcurrants like ruby glass beads. The ivy trailing around each tier sets off the creamy chocolate beautifully and the scarlet roses and petals scattered around the table all pick up the red of the fruits.

"Where's the cake knife?" I ask Laurence.

"I haven't seen it." He looks flummoxed.

"Oh, no. It was on the hall table."

Unlike the other 99 million things we have brought over, we have apparently forgotten the beautiful crystal cake knife. I feel so sorry for Olivia, who had gone to so much trouble to get this gift delivered to us in good time. I have a whispered word with her and try to explain that although we have to use a substitute today, we'll use the crystal knife and server for many years. Somehow, it doesn't sound good enough.

I have a perfect view from our table of all our guests as they easily find their places, and of the caterers waiting in anticipation at the long buffet tables. Jonathan kindly says a brief grace and we begin our meal. Our first course is served and I choose the goats cheese crostini.

Next, I sample a little of everything from the buffet tables and the highlights are the plump langoustines that accompany the delicious salmon and the hot, cheese-melting wholemeal pie stuffed with ratatouille. That's not to say that the rest isn't delightful. The beef is tender and dark pink, the chicken sweet and moist in a lemon cream dressing and the spinach roulade a colourful mix of red peppers, green base and melting mozzarella. I don't even sample the hot new potatoes and steamed asparagus. At last I understand why Leonie had insisted on larger plates… Meanwhile, our waitresses ensure that all of our guests have a constantly replenished supply of wines and soft drinks.

6.30PM: I check the time on Laurence's watch as I've followed tradition by not wearing mine. How has it got so late? Even though my Time Plan is far away at home, I can feel it pulling us with invisible strings. "The evening guests will be here in an hour," I whisper. "I think we'd better start the poems." Despite Laurence's calm reaction I feel complete anguish for him. I am so, *so* relieved that I've opted out of any public speaking. Now our day has arrived I want to enjoy every second – not suffer the jelly legs of stage fright. I can see Laurence's plastic folder of poems and scrawled notes on the table and privately swear eternal gratitude to him for taking this on.

THE WEDDING FEAST

THE SPEECHES

No other part of a wedding day is so heavily loaded with dread and expectations as the Speeches:

- Traditionally, the speeches take place after the last course of the meal and before the cake is cut. The usual order is bride's father (or giver away), then groom and, finally, best man.
- The first and most important rule is to keep speeches short. Allow five minutes maximum per speaker.
- Insist that speeches will not offend or embarrass. Politely request that speakers do a timed practice run. Reassure nervous speakers that a few words of thanks and a raised glass will be just fine if they lose their nerve.
- If you truly don't want speeches, don't have them. Be aware, however, that for some guests there may be a sense of anticlimax.
- Consider switching roles around. Your headmistress mum might be better able to kick off the proceedings than your retiring father. Uncles, friends, sisters, yourself or anyone with a talent for public speaking may be a better choice than the traditional speech givers.
- Consider alternatives that better express your personalities and wedding theme. Commission a professional or ask a friend to perform a poem or song about you. A hired stand-up comedian should be much funnier than your best man (but do check out the material first).

Professional speechwriters will provide coaching, or write a speech, or cover both for about £200.

As soon as our guests' main course is cleared, Laurence stands up. The room falls silent. My limbs are paralysed and I drop my head and clench my fingers as he speaks a short preamble. He refers to the long-running family joke – that his Auntie Edna would bring her own sandwiches to the wedding if he ever married. That elicits a laugh as well as providing an opportunity to thank our generous caterers. Introducing the poetry, he recalls that his art college friends will now be getting worried as during his Dadaist period one of his epics was titled, 'The Larval Loin-Headed Anti-Christ Meets Mother Teresa On An Off Day.' Well, that gets a laugh as well. To my amazed ears, he not only sounds calm and assured but is also holding the room rapt like a professional. Well, then again, I suppose he is a professional lecturer! Nevertheless, I'm astonished. Then, turning to me, he begins to read his own poem, 'Jewel'. As he reads the last verse his intense blue eyes lock onto mine and the whole room listens in silence:

'And most of all, most real of all,
The poetry that is you that colours my soul,
Yet philosophy can no more express without flaw,
My love, than this poem, my song for the jewel I adore.'

This public declaration of love is one aspect of the wedding that I had given no thought to before the event. Laurence's poem, read in such a public manner, stirs my emotions so deeply that it hurts. I'm aware of the sudden power of his gaze in front of the attentive crowd, like a piercing spotlight. Today is the perfect coming together of the private and public, the religious and romantic.

Next, our friend from Accrington rises and reads John Cooper Clarke's 'I Wanna' (yes, he did find a copy) – and it's brilliant, as are his two self-penned poems. Next, Gwen reads my amended version of a 'Recipe for a Wedding Cake' that again impresses everyone and she finishes with a lovely surprise blessing in Welsh. Finally, Ed reads superbly from Sir Walter Scott's 'Lay of the Last Minstrel', an extract on the meaning of love. Laurence stands again and gives his thank yous (or what should have been mine). As he thanks Lorraine, his own mum and my mum, I scurry over with elaborate hand tied bouquets and give each surprised recipient a kiss. Finally, the caterers deliver glasses of pink champagne to everyone, and Keith stands and proposes a toast to "the Bride and Groom!"

There are more photographs and applause as we cut the cake – dessert can now be served. Suddenly, there is a crisis. Leonie shows me a wedge of cake topped with scoops of ice cream, and a portion of juicy red fruits all awash with chocolate sauce – and a burnt-out stub of sparkler. When the staff light the sparklers they only burn for a few seconds and die. Don't bother, I tell her.

Later, she tells me the waitresses served the dessert and then asked if guests wanted the sparkler lit. They then lit them at the table, giving a total of about 5 seconds sparkling excitement.

7.20PM: As we finish dessert, John suggests we catch the last of the light for some formal photographs out in the churchyard. I just have time to ask Laurence's (and now my) cousin Dawn to hand out the lucky bags to the children. Then, happy to forego coffee, Laurence and I slip outside.

"You know," I say, feeling swept along by the warmth of emotion and well-wishing from all our friends and family around us, "this is the happiest day of my life."

"It's the happiest day of my life, too," he replies, squeezing my arm and leaning over to kiss me. Forty-eight hours ago, who would have expected us to say that?

Outside, the village is paling in the dying light; the sky a wash of pearly grey and pink that softens the rounded hedges, steep roofs and barley-twist chimneys of the silent village. Meeting old friends and family arriving for the evening, I know we must not stay away for long. Beside the romantic ruin of Eccleston's former church, we pose for some portrait photographs. It is getting chilly now but at last we are almost alone and can hold hands and stare into each other's eyes without a crowd milling around us.

8.10PM: Back at the hall everything feels rather messy. The band have set up their gear but are sitting on the edge of the stage drinking beer. Keith and Fran are trying their best to make space for the dancing but I meet a guest with a coffee cup in her hand complaining that she has nowhere to sit. We discuss a different layout so people don't lose their seats. The final arrangement is perfect, with seating around the edge of the dance floor for guests to watch or take breaks. My nephew Alexander asks if he can light the candles at the tables. The scent of vanilla rises into the air as the candles flare to life and our guests settle down again in the candlelight.

8.30PM: At last the dancing has begun and I've taken the lead along with Laurence in an English country dance. As predicted, it's a hoot, especially when it gets complex and we're 'do-si-do-ing', skipping through arches of upstretched arms and galloping around. I want to hug everyone in the room and the dancing gives me a chance to waltz against hot chests, take slippery hands in a circle and laugh at all our strange cavorting. I'm relieved that there are enough couples volunteering to have a go, and over the night almost everyone gets up for a boogie.

9.15PM: An abundance of cheeses – brie, blue cheese and local Cheshire – have been set out on large wooden boards. The French bread, biscuits, celery and black and green grapes are all of the best quality. The final tier of wedding cake is also on display and people have been hacking away at that, too. Wandering together, Laurence and I experience the pleasure of the moment. I love the chatter and movement of it all; the tints of pink, crimson and gold, the tiny flames of fire on the candelabra, the people passing outside the entrance craning their necks to see inside the glowing hall. Unexpectedly, it is the children who utterly surrender to the symbols and celebration. Outside, the bridesmaids and my new nephew David are spinning a story of ghosts and ghouls in the candlelight, shrieking and whispering as the trees darken in the twilight. They are devising a play, they tell us. Returning to the heat and motion, there is Eleonor in a golden dress running towards us with hair streaming backwards. One year old Thomas totters back and forth across the dance floor, fascinated by the rhythmic mass of dancers.

10.20PM: A small crisis at the beer pump. Keith and friends Pete and Aitch have decided to man the beer pump and serve people drinks as the area was getting too congested. Over on the dance floor there is growing evidence of the free bar and its effects – when the band start to play some pop standards the dance floor is packed. Babies, children, young and old are all dancing together. My Dutch Auntie is doing some kind of wild hippie dance. My brother-in-law Nick is jiving like a pro. The high point for me has to be seeing my own 75 old mum get up and dance. Go, Mum go!

Later, Laurence and I dance to a slow number, wrapped in each other's arms. His arms feel hot and strong and tight around me and I lean my head on his shoulder. We didn't manage our first dance to Van Morrison's 'Queen of the Slipstream' (our rehearsal, waltzing around our living room made me cry too much) but this, unwatched and private, is even better.

11.15PM: Taxis are arriving and farewells are being taken. Again, the Time Plan pops up in my brain and I know it's time to make a gracious farewell. The party is still humming with chatter and goodbyes as we leave while everything is at this highpoint. Now we can truly enjoy the fruits of our pre-planning as we leave Keith and his friends to pay the band and lock up while our ushers collect mementos.

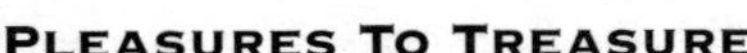

PLEASURES TO TREASURE

MEMORIES

- On the Big Day give a friend a list of mementos to collect. Otherwise your precious confetti, place cards, champagne corks, buttonholes and table decorations may all be swept away with the rubbish.
- Guest books also need to be delegated to a trusted usher or friend to capture congratulation messages on paper on the day.
- After the wedding, set aside mementoes in a storage box (*Rose covered box, stationers: £4*). Your memory box might also hold dress swatches, your tiara, scrapbooks, copies of the speeches and even those dreaded To Do lists.

As the cold night air hits my bare arms, sweet relief keeps me warm and glowing. The wedding has been a success. There have been no disasters, accidents or gaffes. Compliments from our guests have been almost ceaseless – about the wedding service, the village, the hall, the food and our own personal efforts. We have been a success. We have publicly sworn our love. And on top of all of this – we are married.

Back at home we sit down in our outfits feeling dazed. Around us lie discarded champagne glasses, torn envelopes, unopened gifts and scrunched up gift wrap. It has been marvellous, we agree. The idea of travelling to a hotel or luxurious first night experience has no appeal at all. It is perfect to be home, just to wander up our own stairs and sleep together in our own bed. After all, we have all the cleaning and clearing to do tomorrow, and then all the hired goods and outfits to return the next day. In fact, I have a whole To Do List still to tackle. And then in three days…Jamaica! Bliss on wings, I think, as I drift off to sleep curled up with Laurence. We'll have a whole week to relive our wedding day in perfect, pampered luxury.

My Unforgettable Moments

1. Waking up to white fluffy clouds high in the sunny blue sky
2. Seeing my hair, make-up and dress for the first time in my bedroom mirror
3. The colourful crowd milling outside the church as I arrived
4. Waiting with Chris with thumping heart at the church door

5 Exchanging gold rings as we spoke our vows
6 Approaching the High Altar, hand in hand, on life's symbolic journey
7 The lawns and trees dappled in golden sunshine as we left the church
8 The beautiful food in such abundance
9 My cake crowned with summer fruits and roses
10 Laurence's speech and his poem 'Jewel'
11 Laurence saying that it was the happiest day of his life
12 Ceilidh dancing in my wedding dress
13 Romantic photos alone in the twilight
14 A long smooching slow dance in Laurence's arms
15 Getting home and the relief hitting us – we'd done it!

ONE WEEK LATER

THE PRICELESS PARTS

We're at the Richmond Inn and the golden lights of Montego Bay twinkle below us in an arc around the beach. The sun is dropping into the ocean like a fireball of crimson and gold. Sipping two banana cabanas (delicious iced banana, Tia Maria and rum), we relax in the balmy heat. Our honeymoon has been quite extraordinary, from the very first moment that we arrived at our villa suite, when a series of white and blue frescoed rooms were revealed to us: a vast bathroom, dressing room, bedroom with double Jacuzzi and balcony. And that was before I noticed a staircase beside our front door.

"There's a *downstairs*," I shouted. Stumbling with jetlag we marvelled at another suite of huge rooms – a luxury kitchen, second bathroom, impeccably furnished lounge and sunbathing terrace overlooking the plantation and ocean. The Tryall Club is not a hotel – it's a network of privately owned villas whose residents enjoy a clubhouse atmosphere and employ an army of staff to cook, clean, drive and caddy.

Our cook, Winsome, serves us a tray of Blue Mountain coffee each morning before dishing up plates of perfumed papaya, pineapple and mango followed by a spicy Jamaican breakfast of savoury yellow ackee and salty swordfish. We are in a heaven where the golf course hugs the sugar-white beach and turquoise ocean while inland lies the primeval sugar plantation, dense with scissor fringed palms, lipstick pink bougainvillea and thick scents of tobacco and banana. This lush jungle is ours to explore in our motorised golf cart, a midget two-seater that trundles up paths far into the green swathes where the stars shine like lanterns in the tropical night. We've barely dragged ourselves away from Tryall until now, only going rafting on the Great River and peering around crumbling plantation houses hidden up potholed tracks high in the steamy hills.

Of course, packing was frantic, given that we left on Wednesday after two days of hectic cleaning and returning hired goods. I will never forget Sunday and the amazing generosity of our friends. Everyone turned up (Keith, Fran, Chris, Lorraine, Aitch, Pete, Liz, and Yvonne) to clean and clear, leaving us barely any work to do except start the long and delightful process of opening our mountain of gifts.

It's been said that if you remember your passport, credit cards and ticket you have all you really need for a great holiday. Yet some things I've brought along are so perfect that they deserve a mention.

SO GLAD I REMEMBERED...

- A couple of good, bumper books to read under the coconut shade on the beach
- Silk honeymoon negligee
- Pink movie star eye mask and earplugs for siestas and flights
- Good sunglasses to cope with the super-bright tropical sunshine
- Swimsuits and tropical sarongs

- Mosquito bite cream
- Digital camera and battery charger
- My husband – especially for those foam fights in the Jacuzzi…

It's not surprising that we both forget things. A few were actually irritating, so here goes:

WISHED THEY WERE HERE…

- Mosquito repellent and mosquito coils (even in Paradise the little blighters love a nibble)
- Fake tan (to cover up the bites)
- Pens and paper to make spontaneous notes
- More dollars in small notes – this army of staff requires a king's ransom in tips.

Tonight we've dragged ourselves away from the resort to see Mo-Bay from a different perspective and reflect on our wedding day now one week has passed. How do we feel? We identify three strands of emotion: overwhelming relief, a sense of accomplishment and a powerful feeling of luck.

RELIEF – We both think the wedding went better than we ever expected. Not only have we already had a surprising number of enthusiastic thank you cards and messages, but we also both experienced an amazing euphoria all through our wedding day. None of the horrors on my dread list happened and neither did any of the more free-floating anxieties in Laurence's head occur. Since

arriving in Jamaica, he has been mildly bothered by wishes that he could reperform his speech but I feel serenely laid back about the whole thing. I tell Laurence his poem and ad lib were marvellous and so many other people have agreed that he'll soon forget all about it.

My own sanity-threatening stress is already fading away into a figment of memory. Yet I'm sure that when I reread this journal I'll have to confront the agony and sleepless nights. Did the success of the day justify that anguish? Today, we'd certainly say that it does. I've also jotted down an account of our spending (How Our Wedding Added Up, Appendix 3) and got over the shock. On the positive side, we cut the average wedding bill in half but we paid for that the hard way – in time, ceaseless work in the final month, and a certain amount of mental torment.

What we've ultimately gained is far more than a cash saving. We, and our friends and families, made a day unique to us. We could never place a price on that.

ACCOMPLISHMENT – We both still feel pretty high from a sense of accomplishment. After all, neither of us had ever planned a big party before and yet together we pulled off a huge event for nearly 90 people. In the end we both worked far harder than we had ever anticipated. The wonder of it all was seeing the various parts come together into a seamless whole. As Chris observed, when our friends, brewery, florist, caterers and furniture hire firm all turned up in sequence on the Friday, it was like pieces of a jigsaw that all magically slotted together in one moment of time. I believe the key to much of our accomplishment was using good suppliers. We are both happy with the way we mixed hiring goods, doing it ourselves, buying cheaply and then splashing out on the crucial aspects. Our Best Buys list therefore contains both very cheap goods alongside a couple of crucially expensive items:

BEST BUYS

	£
Wedding dress hire	250
Tiara	15
Four large flower hanging baskets	60
Invitations, Orders of Service, menus	25
Two bridesmaids' dresses	100
Furniture hire for 70	264
Hall hire	225
Wallpaper, silk flowers, candelabra	Guest contribution
Bridal car	Guest contribution
Personal Shopper	Free
Wedding gift service	Free
Jamaica honeymoon	Prize
Wine and champagne	Prize
Caterer	2,300

Our final Best Buy cost more than all of the rest put together – the caterer. At a whopping £2,300 it feels hard to justify that amount as a Best Buy. Yet for that sum we got fresh and generous amounts of top quality local food, heavy brocaded linen and napkins, professional waitress service, cake decoration, spotless high class crockery, corkage, ice buckets, glasses and cutlery, plus that indefinable 'X' factor – peace of mind. A snip, in my estimation, at £2,300. Plus, in the frantic run up to the honeymoon, we and all our friends were still feasting on the beautifully wrapped and refrigerated buffet from Sunday through to Tuesday.

LUCK – Sitting on the Richmond Inn terrace with no worries beyond asking our driver to take us on to our restaurant for dinner, it's easy to dismiss the element of luck. After all, hadn't I organised (or maybe overorganised) the day to perfection? Yet all the micromanagement in the world can't make the sun shine from a clear blue sky, or stop family and friends from suffering accidents or illness. So I believe luck is a factor in a successful wedding. Our lingering euphoria is not so much about best buys and budgets, as remembering those parts of the wedding that it is impossible to put a price on – because money can't ever buy them.

THE PRICELESS PARTS

- Laurence using his talents for art, design and photography
- Making my own confetti from our own roses
- A timeless wedding service, made unique to us
- The sheer graft of all our helpers in decorating, organising and cleaning
- Emotional waves of goodwill from our guests that supported and steered the whole day along
- My sister's imagination and dedication
- Sunshine
- Chris on my arm and by my side
- My dad and my sister's performance
- Keeping this journal
- Luck! It all fell into place
- Never, ever, doubting the rightness of marrying each other

Sitting on this terrace overlooking the Caribbean Sea, I know I am a lucky woman. I understand that we spend so much of our lives with our inner hopes hidden in murky depths of daily worry and frustration. For most of us, it takes toil and determination to get what we truly want and need. Then suddenly the perfect configuration strikes; the sun breaks through the cloud and our smothered inner selves surface and connect with the warmth and goodness of others. It is those few moments that crystallise as happy memories; that make a life worth living and keep our spirits strong and shining for the rest of our lives.

Now I have Laurence beside me I see the world not just through my own eyes, but also from the shared perspective of two people in love. The wedding is over and like all brides I know I will miss the froth and frills and flowers. Yet now at last, we are free to build on the shared foundation of our wedding with a tender understanding of each other's weaknesses and stronger admiration for our mutual strengths. Getting up to stroll through the heady bougainvillea to the car, I rejoice that here stands the man most suited to me in the entire world, slipping his hand into mine in the darkness. We have a lifetime before us, launched from our unique day. The wedding is over. Our journey through life is just beginning.

APPENDIX 1

TIME PLAN

ACTION	WHERE, WHEN, WHO	NOTES AND PROPS
MONDAY 18TH		
Final visit	2pm village hall *Laura, Laurence, Keith, Leonie*	Final checklist Menu
FRIDAY 22ND		
Final checks	Phone caterer, furniture hire, florist, brewery *Laura*	Check final details
TUESDAY 26TH		
Pick up dress	Annie's Brides *Laura*	Closes 5.15pm
Infomal photos	Dress details, decorations *Laura, Laurence*	Digital camera
Make ganache	*Laura*	Refrigerate
WEDNESDAY 27TH		
Beauty treatment	9.30am Salon *Laura*	
Cakes from freezer	*Laura*	Add liqueur
Wedding rehearsal	6.30pm *Laura, Laurence, Keith, Liz, Yvonne Nicola, Angela, Chris, Jonathan, Fran, Derek*	Orders of Service/poems
Pay for service	*Laurence*	Cash

ACTION	WHERE, WHEN, WHO	NOTES AND PROPS
THURSDAY 28TH		
Pick up hall keys	9.30am Jill's house *Laura, Lorraine*	Request spares
Set up hall	*Laura, Lorraine, Laurence*	Fridges/ freezers on Boxes to hall
Pick up mens' suits	Pronuptia *Keith*	All paid
Pick up cake stands	Cake shop *Laura*	
Gift delivery	4-9pm home *Laura*	
Finish cakes	Evening *Laura*	Refrigerate
FRIDAY 29TH		
Set up hall	*Lorraine, Laura, Yvonne, Liz, Keith, Laurence, Fran, Chris*	
Exhibition	*Laurence*	
Cake to hall	*Laura*	Fridge ready
Hired furniture	Noon delivery *Events Solution*	
Beer cask	Noon delivery *Weetwood Beers*	Low table
Flowers	Afternoon *Sue*	Church open
Caterer set up	4pm *Leonie*	
SATURDAY 30TH		
Caterer set up	10am *Leonie*	Spare keys
Hairdresser	10am Farndon *Laura, Hilary, Helen*	Tiara
Garden furniture	11am hall lawn *Keith, Laurence, Chris*	Sun shade if hot

ACTION	WHERE, WHEN, WHO	NOTES AND PROPS
Bride's flowers	1.30pm Home *Sue*	
Church flowers	2pm church *Sue*	
Bride's car	2pm home *Laura, Lorraine, Nick, Chris*	Car decoration
Informal photos	2pm home *Chris*	Digital camera
Formal photos	2pm hall *John*	Copy schedule to ushers
Arrival at church	2.30pm *Laurence, Keith, Fran, Liz, Yvonne*	Orders of Service Poems Buttonholes Bridesmaids' flowers Confetti/ bubbles
Rings	2.30pm *Laurence to Keith*	
Bridesmaids	2.30pm hall *Nicola, Angela, Helen, Hilary*	
Bride to church	2.45pm *Nick, Lorraine, Chris, Laura*	
Arrival photos	2.55pm church *John*	Photography schedule
Wedding Service	3pm church	Orders of Service
Collection	Church door *Alexander*	
Bubbles	Church door *Alexander, David*	Photography schedule
Confetti	At gates *everyone*	Photography schedule

ACTION	WHERE, WHEN, WHO	NOTES AND PROPS
Flower transfer	Church to hall *Sue*	
Drinks	4pm – hall lawn *caterers*	In hall if rain
Guest Book	Hall *Liz, Yvonne*	Circulate
Gifts	Gift Table *ushers*	
Dinner	5pm Hall *caterers*	Menus and placecards
Grace	*Jonathan*	
Music	*Ushers*	Music system, CDs
Poems	6.30-ish *Laurence, Martin, Gwen, Ed*	Spare copies
Bouquets	Present to Lorraine and mums *Laura*	Bouquets
Cake cutting	*Laura, Laurence*	Knife
Toast	*Keith, Caterers*	Pink champagne
Tables moved	7pm *Keith and helpers*	Light candles
Evening guests	7.30pm *Laura/Laurence greet*	
Band arrive	7.30pm *Keith*	As contract
First set	8pm *Devil's Fire*	
Interval	9.15pm refreshments *caterers*	Interval CD
Second set	9.45pm *Devil's Fire*	
Band ends	11pm pay band *Keith*	Cheque
Taxis	11pm onwards	
Farewells	11-11.30pm *Laura and Laurence*	

ACTION	WHERE, WHEN, WHO	NOTES AND PROPS
Finish	11.30pm *Keith, ushers*	Candles out, lock up
SUNDAY 31ST		
Clear hall	Afternoon *Keith, ushers, Chris, Laura*	Retrieve food and drink
	Laurence	Retrieve mementos
Thank you meal	Evening home *all helpers*	Beer/buffet
MONDAY 1ST SEPTEMBER		
Return items	Hall keys, cake stands, dress *Laura*	
	Men's suits *Keith*	
	Marjorie's hat *Laurence*	
TUESDAY 2ND		
Holiday cash	Pick up from bank *Laura*	
Pack	Pack bags *Laurence, Laura*	Holiday list
WEDNESDAY 3RD		
Honeymoon	Check in 14.25 Manchester	Passports
	Drop off *Chris*	Tickets

APPENDIX 2
EMERGENCY KIT

Best man

Mobile phone
Contact details of all suppliers
Time Plan
Guest list
Seating plans
Cash or cheques
Insurance policy details
Taxi details
Superglue and scissors
Pens and notepad
Duplicate speeches
First-aid kit
And don't forget the rings!

Bride and Bridesmaids

Touch-up make-up
Hairspray
Kirby grips
Safety pins
Tissues
Spare tights
Nail file
Needle and thread
Feminine supplies
Headache tablets
Breath freshener
If all else fails – a radiant smile

APPENDIX 3
HOW OUR WEDDING ADDED UP

(Figures in italics are estimates)

	JAN	JULY	SEPT	NATIONAL AVERAGE
Engagement ring	500	500	500	1,095
Bride's wedding ring	*100*	*100*	200	296
Groom's wedding ring	*100*	*100*	245	280
Parties (hen and stag)	0	0	100	449
Bride's dress	*300*	250	250	921
Bride's shoes	0	50	50	86
Veil	0	0	0	97
Headdress	15	15	15	81
Bridesmaid's outfits	*100*	100	100	383
Bride's jewellery	0	0	42	119
Grooms/mens' outfits	*150*	240	370	197
Lingerie	0	25	63	99
Beauty	0	0	160	82
Hairdressing	*45*	*45*	45	78
Flowers	*350*	*350*	588	481
Transport	0	0	0	364
Ceremony fees	*200*	*400*	427	319
Stationery	0	0	25	224
Photography	*400*	*685*	685	766
Video	0	0	0	493
Reception hire	*350*	*464*	489	1215
Catering	*700*	*1,500*	2,300	2,447
Drinks/wine	*640*	*640*	783	1,049
Wedding cake	*100*	*100*	100	240

	JAN	JULY	SEPT	NATIONAL AVERAGE
Favours/decorations	0	*100*	175	143
Music	*350*	*525*	525	421
Going away outfit	0	0	0	133
Thank you gifts	0	20	100	208
First night hotel	0	0	0	170
Honeymoon	*500*	*500*	500	2,828
TOTALS	*4,900*	*6,709*	8,837	15,764
SUBTRACT				
Guest contributions			1,100	
Prizes			640	
TOTAL WEDDING SPEND			**7,197**	**15,764**

USEFUL WEBSITES

There are plenty of great resources on the Web whether you're looking for a photographer, finding out about church weddings, buying a wedding dress, designing your own invitations, writing your own vows, or preparing in any other way for your big day.

I've put together a personal list of the best resources currently available online. You can find this list at **www.whiteladder-press.com**. Posting the list on the website means we can keep it updated. We also hope that you'll let us know of any other websites that you think should be added.

You can also see some of our wedding photographs on the web at www.wedding diaries.co.uk.

CONTACT US

You're welcome to contact White Ladder Press if you have any questions or comments for either us or the author. Please use whichever of the following routes suits you.

Phone: **01803 813343 between 9am and 5.30pm**
Email: **enquiries@whiteladderpress.com**
Fax: **01803 813928**
Address: **White Ladder Press, Great Ambrook, Near Ipplepen, Devon TQ12 5UL**
Website: **www.whiteladderpress.com**

WHAT CAN OUR WEBSITE DO FOR YOU?

If you want more information about any of our books, you'll find it at **www.whiteladderpress.com**. In particular you'll find extracts from each of our books, and reviews of those that are already published. We also run special offers on future titles if you order online before publication. And you can request a copy of our free catalogue.

Many of our books also have links pages, useful addresses and so on relevant to the subject of the book. You'll also find out a bit more about us and, if you're a writer yourself, you'll find our submission guidelines for authors. So please check us out and let us know if you have any comments, questions or suggestions.

Full Time Father

HOW TO SUCCEED AS A STAY AT HOME DAD

"At last, a hands-on, amusing and above all realistic guide for dads who have given up work to bring up their children. What makes this book so rewarding is that it is written by a father who has been there, seen it and done it."

Nick Cavender, Chairman, HomeDad UK

So your partner earns more than you do?
You've been made redundant? You hate the job?
Being a full time dad can make a lot of sense.

But isn't it a bit weird? Actually no; it's a growing trend. Nearly one in ten fathers in the UK now takes the main responsibility for looking after the kids, often full time.

It's a big decision though. What will your mates think? Will you ever get a decent job again? Won't you miss the cut and thrust of the office? And won't you go stark staring mad without any mental stimulation too sophisticated for a toddler? It's not just you, either. It's the whole family set up. Who wears the trousers? Who controls the family purse? And does it mean you have to clean the house and do the shopping, too?

Full Time Father is written by a stay at home dad and draws on his survey of other 'homedads' as well as on his own experience. It examines all the key issues, passes on masses of valuable tips and advice, and lets the reader know what to expect – both good and bad – should they decide to become a homedad themselves.

£9.99

THE VOICE OF TOBACCO

"An amazing new book on smoking – it has great style and humour, and is brilliantly funny. Read this happy smoker's guide – if only I had been the author."
LESLIE PHILLIPS

What does the Voice of Tobacco say to you?
There's no need to give up; just cutting down will do.
How can it be bad for you when it feels so good?
Just one cigarette can't hurt you, now can it?

It's hard not to listen. Especially when, from the other side of the debate, we smokers have all been lectured by self-righteous prigs who think that (a) we should want to give up and (b) giving up smoking should be easy.

Well we don't and it ain't.

And yet there does come a time when, no matter how much we enjoy smoking, we have to become not smokers.

Richard Craze's guide gives it to you straight: what it's really like to give up smoking. The headaches, the sleeplessness, the irritability. And The Voice. He's been there and his diary reports back from the front line. It may not be pleasant, but it's honest. It may or may not help you to give up smoking, but it will certainly get you looking at smoking in a new way. And it will give you something to do with your hands.

This is the diary of a dedicated and happy smoker who is now not smoking. Here's how he did it. Here's how to do it without the trauma, the withdrawal symptoms, the twitching, the bad temper. Yeah, right. In your dreams.

£6.99

The White Ladder Diaries

"To start a business from scratch with a great idea but little money is a terrifying but thrilling challenge. White Ladder is a fine example of how sheer guts and drive can win the day."
TIM WATERSTONE

Have you ever dreamed of starting your own business?

Want to know what it's like? I mean, what it's really like?

Ros Jay and her partner, Richard Craze, first had the idea for White Ladder Press in the summer of 2002. This is the story of how they overcame their doubts and anxieties and brought the company to life, for only a few thousand pounds, and set it on its way to being a successful publishing company (this is its third book).

The White Ladder Diaries isn't all theory and recollections. It's a real life, day-by-day diary of all those crucial steps, naïve mistakes and emotional moments between conceiving the idea for a business and launching the first product. It records the thinking behind all the vital decisions, from choosing a logo or building a website, to sorting out a phone system or getting to grips with discounts.

What's more, the diary is littered with tips and advice for anyone else starting up a business. Whether you want to know how to register a domain name or how to write a press release, it's all in here.

If they could do it, so can you. Go on – stop dreaming.
Be your own boss.

£9.99

ORDER FORM

You can order any of our books via any of the contact routes on page 203, including on our website. Or fill out the order form below and fax it or post it to us.

We'll normally send your copy out by first class post within 24 hours (but please allow five days for delivery). We don't charge postage and packing within the UK. Please add £1 per book for postage outside the UK.

Title (Mr/Mrs/Miss/Ms/Dr/Lord etc) ______________________________

Name ______________________________

Address ______________________________

____

Postcode ______________________________

Daytime phone number ______________________________

Email ______________________________

No. of copies	Title	Price	Total £
Postage and packing £1 per book (outside the UK only):			
TOTAL:			

Please either send us a cheque made out to White Ladder Press Ltd or fill in the credit card details below.

Type of card ☐ Visa ☐ Mastercard ☐ Switch

Card number ______________________________

Start date (if on card) __________ Expiry date __________ Issue no (Switch) __________

Name as shown on card ______________________________

Signature ______________________________

INDEX